VGM Careers for You Series

## CAREERS FOR

# HEALTH NUTS

# & Others Who Like to Stay Fit

## BLYTHE CAMENSON

### SECOND EDITION

### *VGM Career Books*

Chicago   New York   San Francisco   Lisbon   London   Madrid   Mexico City
Milan   New Delhi   San Juan   Seoul   Singapore   Sydney   Toronto

The **McGraw·Hill** Companies

**Library of Congress Cataloging-in-Publication Data**

Camenson, Blythe.
    Careers for health nuts & others who like to stay fit / Blythe Camenson— 2nd ed.
       p.   cm.  — (VGM careers for you series)
      ISBN 0-07-140899-1 (alk. paper)
       1. Allied health personnel—Vocational guidance.   I. Title: Careers for health
nuts and others who like to stay fit.   II. Title.   III. VGM careers for you series.

R697.A4C35  2003
610.69'53—dc21                                     2003053762

1 2 3 4 5 6 7 8 9 0   LBM/LBM   2 1 0 9 8 7 6 5 4 3

ISBN 0-07-140899-1

McGraw-Hill books are available at special quantity discounts to use as premiums and
sales promotions, or for use in corporate training programs. For more information, please
write to the Director of Special Sales, Professional Publishing, McGraw-Hill,
Two Penn Plaza, New York, NY 10121-2298. Or contact your local bookstore.

This book is printed on acid-free paper.

*To Deborah Gordon and Andy Harper,*
*the nicest health nuts I know*

# Contents

# Acknowledgments

The author would like to thank the following health nuts for providing information about their careers:

| | |
|---|---|
| John Berberich | Sports Psychologist |
| Kent Brinkley | Landscape Architect/Garden Historian |
| Theresa Bulmer | Store Manager |
| Bobbie Campbell | Sports Medicine Nurse |
| Frank Cassisa | Certified Personal Trainer |
| Beverly Citron | Assistant Cruise Director |
| Helen Cox | Occupational Therapist |
| Laurie DeJong | Physical Therapist |
| Emily Friedland | Dietitian |
| Loretta Hodyss | Extension Agent |
| Richard Mattson | Professor/Horticultural Therapist |
| Nancy McVicar | Health Writer |
| Sally Miller | Manager of Food Cooperative |
| Stephie Morin | Certified Nurse-Midwife |
| Brad Potts | Nurse Practitioner |
| Regina Renteria | Counselor, Educator |
| Nancy Stevenson | Horticultural Therapist |
| Carol Stull | Grower |
| Roy Upton | Herbalist |
| Rob Verner | Psychiatric Nurse |

# CHAPTER ONE

# Jobs for Health Nuts

ealth nuts are not necessarily, as the term may imply, fanatics. Rather, they are people who've made a personal commitment to leading healthier, more productive lifestyles. Health nuts take a variety of paths to improve their lives. They may keep abreast of medical and scientific research and apply the results to their own lives. They may have quit smoking and drinking and are careful with any medications they might have to use, often seeking alternative, natural remedies. They pay attention to the food they eat, how it's grown and prepared, avoiding fats and salt and chemical additives. They practice preventative medicine and see their doctors for regular checkups. They know their cholesterol levels and keep tabs on their blood pressure. They take care of their bodies with daily exercise, walking or jogging or playing tennis. They're interested in psychology, mental health, and spiritual well-being, too.

As the twenty-first century begins, many health nuts are thinking about more than their own bodies and lifestyles; their concern goes beyond their own backyards to the complex world in which we all live. They value the environment and realize that not so long ago we were on a course that would have rapidly destroyed it. They try to do their part—conserving water, carpooling or bicycling to work, and recycling newspapers, plastic, aluminum cans, and glass.

Even more committed are those who strive to combine their love of and concern for good health and the environment into meaningful work and careers. If you are reading this book, you probably see yourself in that last category. You are someone searching for a way to share what you have learned, a way to give back to the earth that supports you.

## Assessing the Options

There are many career options for health nuts, some obvious, some not. The jobs we'll examine in this book might spark your interest or, with a little creative brainstorming, lead you to other related professions. The real people you'll meet within these pages will give you firsthand insights into what it's like working in the various categories of this rewarding field. By contacting the resources listed in the appendixes, you can find even more in-depth information to help with your decision.

But first, let's begin with a little self-assessment. Ask yourself these basic questions:

1. How much time am I willing to invest for education and specialized training?
   __ No formalized training (I can use what I already know)
   __ Two to three months of on-the-job training
   __ One to two years in a technical or associate's degree program
   __ Four years in a bachelor's degree program
   __ One to five years beyond the bachelor's in a master's or doctorate program
2. What kind of work setting would I prefer?
   __ Outdoors
   __ In an office
   __ In a hospital or clinic
   __ In a restaurant
   __ In a gym or health club
   __ In a retail store
   __ In my own home office

3. What kind of employer would I rather work for?
  __ The government
  __ A private corporation or business
  __ A not-for-profit agency
  __ Self-employed
4. Do I prefer to work alone or be part of a team?
5. What is my primary area of interest?
  __ People (__ well people __ sick people)
  __ Food (__ growing __ preparing __ selling)
  __ The environment
6. Do I have good oral and written communication skills?
7. Do I have a love of science and technology?
8. What kind of work do I prefer?
  __ Study and research
  __ Teaching
  __ Hands-on work
9. Am I willing to relocate?
10. Is salary an important consideration?

After you've answered these questions, you have to analyze what your responses imply. A willingness to relocate means that job options are limitless; a desire to stay in one particular area will narrow the opportunities.

Someone who is not interested in science and technology but who has good verbal and communication skills would do well as a writer or educator but not so well as a medical doctor or forest technician. A team player would fare better in a corporate or government setting than someone who prefers to work alone. For the more lucrative professions, a desire for an attractive salary would have to be coupled with a willingness to spend several years studying.

Once you have a good idea of your ideal working conditions, you are ready to take a closer look at some of your career options.

# The Right Career for You

What follows is a breakdown of the career categories that would appeal to health nuts. You can read more about the different job titles in the chapters ahead.

## Healers and Caregivers

Healers and caregivers are nurturers by nature. They are concerned with both the physical and emotional well-being of the people with whom they work.

Some health nuts prefer working with well people; others derive great satisfaction from helping the sick. They work in traditional medical careers or in some that are not so traditional. They spend years studying medicine or nursing or act as counselors, educators, or group facilitators, addressing the many needs of individuals or entire communities.

Work settings are as varied as the careers. Nurturers find employment in hospitals and health clinics, in colleges or childbirth clinics.

Here is a sampling of job titles for health nuts who work as nurturers:

- Nurse-midwives
- Nurse-practitioners
- Sports medicine specialists
- Sports psychologists
- Mental health counselors

## Healing with Plants

Some health nuts train in alternative healing methods, working with herbs or horticulture. They use plants to heal, to teach, and to raise the self-esteem levels of their clients. They find work in private practice or at hospitals, laboratories, or botanical gardens.

Here is a sampling of job titles for health nuts working with the healing properties of plants:

- Herbalists
- Naturopaths
- Pharmacognosy specialists
- Horticultural therapists

## Let's Get Physical

Many health nuts who are concerned with physical fitness find satisfying work helping others reach personal goals. They work in private health clubs, spas, gyms, country clubs, civic centers, or YMCAs. And while most careers in fitness deal with well people, some health nuts prefer working with a physically challenged population, providing rehabilitation therapy. These professionals work in hospitals, clinics, or nursing homes.

Here is a sampling of job titles for health nuts concerned with fitness:

- Personal trainers
- Fitness instructors
- Athletics coaches
- Physical therapists
- Occupational therapists
- Recreational therapists

## The World of Food

Health nuts are well aware of the importance of food to a long and healthy life. They prefer vegetables that are organically grown without harmful pesticides and chemical fertilizers. Some avoid eating red meat; still others are dedicated vegetarians or vegans.

The world of food offers many career options for health nuts. Some find work on small organic farms or with retail food co-ops. Others gravitate toward natural food stores and restaurants. Still others share information with the public, teaching about good nutrition, weight loss, or diet.

Here is a sampling of job titles for health nuts working in the world of food:

- Organic growers
- Organic farm managers
- Cooperative Extension Service agents
- Natural food store sales
- Vegetarian restaurant chefs and servers
- Dietitians and nutritionists
- Health and food inspectors

## The Health Beat

Health and medical issues are of concern to the general public, and most newspapers and many magazines devote space to reports on new developments or trends in the related fields. There are even magazines focused entirely on fitness and lifestyle, and bookstore and library shelves are crammed with books on spiritual and physical wellness. More often than not, self-help and how-to books end up cornering slots on the bestseller list.

Health nuts with good writing skills and a little market savvy can learn how to be a part of this health beat, researching and writing articles and health guides.

Here is a sampling of job titles for health nuts with writing skills:

- Book authors
- Freelancer writers
- Reporters/staff writers
- Columnists
- Investigative reporters
- Lecturers
- Photographers

## Healing the Environment

Some health nuts prefer to work with a more global picture; in other words, these are people who can see the forest through the trees. A healthy body and lifestyle are not enough if the environment we live in is not also healthy.

Those with environmental concerns can find satisfying careers dealing with landscape preservation, environment conservation, wildlife protection, or pollution control.

Although much conservation work takes place out of doors, not all of it does. Drafting tables and computers are as much a part of the field as fire lines and surveying equipment.

Here is a sampling of job titles for health nuts concerned with the environment:

- Landscape architects and designers
- Land planners
- Conservationists
- Foresters
- Forest technicians
- Park rangers
- Environmental engineers

## Dream Jobs for Health Nuts

Job-hunting health nuts dream of finding positions where their skills and interests can be combined. Would any of these help-wanted ads send you racing to the post office to mail off your resume?

- **Assistant Chef.** Collectively run vegetarian eating establishment seeks individual with at least one year's experience working with specialized menus. Some food-serving experience is also desired. Duties include planning meals, ordering produce, and assisting in all phases of food preparation. Basic salary plus profit sharing after one year.
- **Food Co-Op Manager.** Candidate must be experienced in all phases of food retailing with a minimum of five years in a cooperative setting. Duties include supervising paid staff and volunteers, managing public relations, and overseeing budgets and finance.

- **Sports Medicine R.N.** Sports clinic needs experienced R.N. for patient assessment and care. Some on-site work at local sporting events. Good PR skills necessary.
- **Horticultural Therapist.** Veteran's Hospital seeks horticultural therapist in year-round program. Work with disabled veterans in on-grounds vegetable and flower garden. Knowledge of special-access landscaping—raised garden beds, wheelchair ramps—essential.
- **Experienced Therapist.** Women's health center needs an experienced therapist to run support groups, provide individual counseling, and act as a liaison with community organizations. Master's degree in counseling, nursing, or related field required.
- **Water Safety Instructor.** YMCA Summer Day Camp needs full-time instructor. Duties include swimming and boating instruction, some lifeguarding. YMCA or Red Cross certification required.

This is just a small sampling of the work that health nuts can find. In the chapters ahead you will be introduced to many more possibilities.

## Salaries for Health Nuts

Salaries vary widely depending on the field you choose to enter. Medical doctors are known for the large salaries they earn, but their investment in time and money to become M.D.s is equally large. Some categories of R.N.s earn salaries almost equal to a doctor's, while other health nuts might work for an hourly wage.

The region in which you work also determines salaries. The northeast and west coast typically pay higher wages than other parts of the country, but the cost of living is higher, too.

Self-employed health nuts—freelance writers or personal trainers, for example—can put in as much time as they choose, determining their own income.

No matter the salary, most health nuts report that working in a field they love more than offsets any income considerations.

## The Job Outlook

Interest in health and environment issues has been on the increase in the last two decades or so. More and more people are becoming aware of the need for healthy living in a healthy environment. This awareness has reached to top levels of our government, resulting in legislation for health care and environmental reform. As more and more programs are instituted, more and more jobs will become available.

For those of you still in high school or college, now is a good time to decide what field interests you and pay attention to what the up-and-coming occupations are. Investigating the various options, studying the appropriate courses, and participating in related hands-on internships will prepare you for the plum jobs awaiting ahead.

Career changers can keep on top of new policies and programs and ready themselves in much the same way. Everyone's job outlook is enhanced by a combination of making educated choices and receiving the right kind of training and experience.

# CHAPTER TWO

# Healers and Caregivers

Nothing is more important to some health nuts than to help others achieve and maintain good health. Health nuts who are healers and caregivers treat their patients holistically, focusing on all aspects of a person's well-being. They view the body as a whole and do not separate physical components from emotional or spiritual ones.

The occupations covered in this chapter attract professionals who see their patients as being basically well. This differs from professionals who adhere to a medical model, which tends to categorize patients as being basically sick. Although some medical doctors, for example, might very well be health nuts, for the most part their training and approach to patient care do not fit the overall theme of this book. Because of this, our focus is primarily on careers other than traditional medicine, although a few categories within the traditional nursing profession are covered.

## Nurses as Health Nuts

To choose a career in nursing means you have a special gift. You sincerely care about people and you know how to show those feelings. Nurses love working with people, all kinds of people. Your patients might be rich or poor, young or old, from a variety of backgrounds and cultures.

As a nurse you have a lot of different options open to you. In a traditional hospital setting you might work with newborns and children, in the emergency room, or in the intensive-care unit. You can assist at a birth or during an operation or provide counseling for psychiatric patients. You can also work in a private counseling center or in an elementary school or university infirmary. Some nurses choose to work in their patients' homes or for a sports clinic, aboard a cruise ship, or at a summer camp. Other nurses work in nursing homes or even in prisons. Nurses can also be administrators and educators, directing the care given in a hospital department or teaching future nurses the skills they'll need in this rewarding career.

At present, there are four different ways you can become a registered nurse, or R.N.

1. Through a two-year community college, earning an associate's degree in nursing
2. Through a three-year hospital-based nursing school, earning a diploma
3. Through a four-year university program, resulting in the bachelor of science degree in nursing, or the B.S.N., as it is commonly called
4. Through a generic master's degree in nursing, a two- to three-year program beyond the bachelor's degree

These days, and certainly in the future, the bachelor of science in nursing is considered the minimum qualification for a satisfying career. The two-year associate's degree and the three-year hospital-based diploma programs are very quickly closing down throughout the country and student nurses are being encouraged to enroll in four-year universities. For many nursing specialties, it is also essential to earn a master's degree or an advanced certificate; and for some nurses, those who wish to teach, for example, a doctorate in nursing is required. After your schooling, you will be expected to take a licensing exam for the basic R.N. certification and for any of the various specialty areas you might choose.

# Nurse-Midwives and Nurse-Practitioners

Nurse-midwives approach pregnancy as a normal condition. They emphasize counseling, provide information and support, and have more time to spend with their patients than physicians usually do. A midwife is there with the patient throughout labor, while many physicians are able to attend only the actual birth.

But midwives are trained to recognize complications, and if any should occur, an obstetrician—the physician who is trained to handle these abnormal situations—is consulted, and they work together to ensure the patient's well-being.

The nurse-practitioner profession was originally designed more than thirty years ago to provide health care to those who didn't have access to physicians. And in some settings today, in rural villages, for example, nurse-practitioners are still the only providers. They are legally licensed to prescribe medication in most states and fully trained to fill in for pediatricians, obstetricians, and general practice physicians. In urban areas, practitioners work with physicians, providing a comprehensive health-care package.

Practitioners focus their attention on a patient's common problems, freeing up time for the physician to correct serious ailments. Nurse-practitioners are not as disease-oriented as physicians; they try to prevent diseases, and, if a disease is not readily correctable, they teach patients how to live with it.

## What the Job Is Like

**Nurse-Midwife.** A nurse-midwife is trained in all areas of normal obstetrics, well-woman gynecological care, care of the newborn, and care of normal healthy women throughout the childbearing cycle and afterward, too. In the United States, most midwives work in hospitals, but some work in birthing centers and some do home care.

Many professionals choose to work with a group of other midwives; their midwifery services are under contract with local hospitals and with physician groups. Occasionally midwives may travel to various community-based health centers, but most of the births occur in hospitals.

Here is a typical look at the work of a nurse-midwife. When a pregnancy begins, a woman comes in for prenatal care at the health center. She sees a midwife for her first visit, which should be early on in her pregnancy. The midwife takes a health history and spends time getting to know her, giving her information about the center's service and about her pregnancy. She does some blood work, a physical exam, decides if any tests are needed, makes any referrals—to a nutritionist, for example, or sometimes to a social worker—then schedules the next visit.

During follow-up appointments the midwife asks how the expectant mother is feeling, if the baby's moving yet, listens to the baby's heart, and measures the belly to see how it's growing.

When a patient goes into labor, either the midwife or one of her coworkers meets her at the hospital. The midwife evaluates her baby and her labor with different monitoring devices. The midwife supports her through the different stages of labor—a nurse is there, too, and a doctor is always available in case of complications. And if the woman wants any medication, the midwife is able to give it to her.

After the baby is born, follow-up visits are scheduled to teach the new mother about newborn care and what to expect from her body as she recovers from the delivery.

Delivering a baby can be a difficult time, and the women appreciate the help given them. A close rapport develops with most patients; some come back for their second babies, and the midwife becomes almost a part of the family. But people have their babies all times of the day and night and on weekends. It's possible that you may have to work in the middle of the night—you may lose sleep sometimes and you will put in long hours. But the rewards more than make up for it. You are taking care of women during an important time in their lives, and you see them go from the early stages of pregnancy to motherhood.

**Nurse-Practitioner.** A nurse-practitioner evaluates a patient's total health-care needs. Patients range in age anywhere from two weeks old to elderly. Initially, the nurse-practitioner does a head-to-toe physical and a complete health assessment. If the complaint is complicated and requires complicated intervention, the practitioner can refer the patient to a physician. If it's a common health problem, the practitioner can diagnose and treat it.

One advantage to being a nurse-practitioner is being able to take care of the whole family—the newborns, Mom and Dad, even the extended family—because health care is more than just the individual. Family origins, culture, the beliefs of parents or grand-parents—it's all a big influence. If one person is sick, it affects everybody. When the nurse-practitioner knows what's going on in the family, it helps him or her to deal with all the family members. If a baby is sick, for example, and Grandmother comes in with a health complaint, she might be very upset about the baby and might not be sleeping well.

However, in a busy clinic, there are often too many people to see and not enough time to spend with them, so nurses can feel pulled from all directions. This is a universal problem. So many people need health care and there are currently not enough people and not enough time to take care of everyone in an ideal manner.

## Job Settings

Nurse-midwives and nurse-practitioners find work in city hospitals, clinics, and private doctors' offices; in rural areas, such as on Indian reservations, in Alaska, or in the Appalachian Mountains; or around the world with the armed forces or the foreign service.

They can also, in much the same way a doctor does, set up an office and work in private practice. Some nurse-midwives and nurse-practitioners even make home visits. Nurses who choose to work with families have several different options they can follow.

Even if they run a private practice, they can work as part of a team in hospitals and clinics. Jobs are available in large cities or rural villages—in fact, nurses working with families can find employment almost anywhere. Their patients range from pregnant women and newborn infants to fathers and grandparents and everyone who comes in between.

## Salaries

Because there is a great demand for nurse-midwives and nurse-practitioners, salaries are very high, if not the highest in the nursing profession. (See Table 2.1.) In fact, a midwife or practitioner can go into private practice and make about the same salary as a doctor with a general practice. This can run to six figures but, of course, depends on the area of the country in which you live and how much competition there is. Nurse-midwives currently earn an average $59,000 annually, a great income level on a par with median incomes in many popular suburban areas.

Nurse-midwives or practitioners who join the armed forces start out at a high military rank and receive all the accompanying benefits. Large private companies, such as in the oil or computer industries with a thousand or more employees, prefer to hire

**TABLE 2.1.** Salaries for Trained Nurses and Nurse-Midwives in the United States

| JOB TITLE TITLE | NUMBER OF JOBS | MEDIAN SALARY | HOURLY WAGE |
|---|---|---|---|
| Nurses | 2,239,816 | $52,520 | $25.25 |
| Nurse-midwives | 6,500 | $59,000 | $28.37 |

Sources: Advance for Nursing, Feb. 2003, American Nurses Association (salary figures for nurses based on sample of eight thousand); American Association of Colleges of Nursing (average salary); Association of Certified Nurse-Midwives (number of certified nurse-midwives).

midwives and practitioners rather than M.D.s. They can afford to pay attractive salaries, but they still save money. One caution: health professionals in this field must carry considerable amounts of malpractice insurance.

Still, as one certified nurse-midwife put it, "What could be more rewarding than job satisfaction and good money?"

## The Job Outlook

A national nursing shortage looms. By 2015, "114,000 jobs for full-time R.N.s are expected to go unfilled nationwide," according to the American Association of Colleges of Nursing. The job outlook for nurse-midwives and nurse-practitioners, therefore, is excellent. Advanced practice nursing—including both midwives and nurse-practitioners—is one career category that is expected to grow faster than average in the next five years. With all of the health-care reform being planned, eventually physicians won't make as much money performing normal, routine duties. Their duties will focus on surgery and other complicated procedures, and the skills of nurse-midwives and nurse-practitioners will be utilized more. In essence, costs will be kept down and everyone will save money.

But cost is not the only factor ensuring a good job outlook. There are many regions in the country that don't attract enough physicians. There are also some patient populations, such as the elderly or inner-city teens, that are being neglected. Midwives and practitioners are in even more demand to work in these areas.

## Is This the Right Career for You?

Ask yourself these questions to assess if you have what it takes to make a good nurse-midwife or nurse-practitioner:

- Am I good with my hands?
- Do I enjoy studying science?

- Am I able to keep track of my activities in writing? (Do I keep a journal or diary, for example?)
- Can people read my handwriting?
- Am I willing to learn another language?
- Am I a good listener?
- Am I interested in helping people?
- Can I avoid feeling squeamish at the sight of blood or if someone's in pain?
- Can I make a commitment and follow it through?
- Am I willing to work hard?
- Can I work as part of a team?

## Training

There are different ways to become a midwife. Some medical programs combine an R.N. degree with midwifery training and a master's degree in nursing. If you're not a nurse when you start the program, it takes three years.

You don't have to be a nurse to be a midwife. Midwives who aren't nurses are called lay midwives, or empirical midwives, depending upon the region. They do not have the full training and certification of nurse-midwives. There are restrictions in different states, and noncertified nurse-midwives may not be licensed to the same degree or even legally recognized—it depends on the state. For more information, contact the American College of Nurse-Midwives, listed in Appendix A.

But all nurse-midwives and nurse-practitioners study in special programs above the R.N. or B.S.N., receiving master's degrees and additional training. They also take licensing exams for their specialties.

## Sports Medicine

Sports medicine is a subspeciality of orthopedic medicine and deals primarily with injuries received during athletic activities. Sports medicine doctors are mainly orthopedic surgeons who see patients when it's too late to institute preventative measures. Sports medicine nurses care for patients suffering from strains, sprains, torn ligaments and muscles, fractures, and dislocations. Patients could be Little League shortstops, professional ballet dancers, ice skaters, aerobics exercisers, or marathon runners. Anyone with an active lifestyle can suffer a sports-related injury. It's the job of the sports medicine nurse to take a patient's history, assist the doctor with his or her treatment plan, and educate the patient so future injuries can be avoided.

Sports medicine nurses work in clinics, hospitals, training rooms, rehabilitation centers, outpatient centers, and school infirmaries. Some nurses also work at first aid stations at various sporting events. They often function as part of a team with physicians, surgeons, and physical therapists. (You can read about careers in physical therapy in Chapter 4.)

## What the Job Is Like

Here's a description of a typical day in the life of one sports medicine nurse.

A nurse works in a private enterprise that is owned by a physician and a physical therapist. She works about thirty-six hours a week, typically Monday through Friday, during the hours from 7 A.M. to 5 P.M. When she gets to work she finds a full schedule of patients. She escorts them to the exam rooms, takes histories, and does brief screenings. If necessary, she takes blood pressure readings and interviews them about how they got their injuries. During patient examinations with a doctor, she records everything that's said and takes notes for the patients. After the doctor leaves the room, she reviews everything the doctor told the patient—the diagnosis, the plan for treatment, and what he or she is supposed to do at home. She might provide samples of medication and explain the side effects. If needed she might also give an injection or take an x-ray.

One advantage to this type of job is the hours, which are much more predicable than hospital work. The job is varied;

sports medicine nurses work with different age groups and can incorporate much of the general knowledge learned in the nursing degree program. One downside is that most of the patients are in a hurry to get well. They're anxious to get back to their sports, and they want to get back now, which means you must be firm in advising them against rushing the healing process.

## Training

Sports medicine nurses should have at least an R.N., but a B.S.N. is preferred. It's also a good idea to have some specialized training. Several colleges and universities offer degrees in this field; for a list of these institutions, contact the American College of Sports Medicine (ACSM) at the address given in Appendix A. Programs are open to registered nurses, licensed practical nurses, and others. It's also possible to get a master's degree in sports medicine.

# Counseling and Psychology

As a counselor, you can choose a variety of settings in which to work and a variety of people to see. You can work in a hospital with acute or chronic psychiatric inpatients, for example, or see clients in a clinic or counseling center on an outpatient basis. The work atmosphere and your duties will vary with the setting.

A variety of professionals work in the mental health field. Medical doctors can specialize in psychiatry and then, as psychiatrists, work full-time in a hospital or have a private practice with hospital privileges. This means that they are able to admit any of their patients who might need hospital care.

Registered nurses can also opt for careers as counselors or psychiatric nurses, working in hospitals or clinics. Many study for a master's degree above the B.S.N. Psychologists spend many years in college earning Ph.D.s. They work similarly to some psychiatrists, but they leave the prescribing of medications to the M.D.s. Psychotherapists, social workers, and family therapists usually have master's degrees and work in hospitals or private practice or for government agencies.

Counselors often work in college and university counseling centers, helping students with personal, academic, and career issues.

As a counselor you can work with very emotionally disturbed patients or with patients who are basically well and just need support working through problems. In order to make the right career choice, it is important to understand the type of work you would be doing. Generally, in mental health clinics or health centers, patients—or clients, as they are normally called—have less severe problems, and the opportunities to help and see improvement are greater. You might work with clients going through a divorce or grieving over the loss of a child or a spouse.

In a hospital, on the other hand, you deal with all types of short- and long-term patients. Many of them could be chronically ill without much hope for improvement. They could be severely depressed, suicidal, or violent—not able to function in their normal lives. Because the medical model often functions vigorously at psychiatric hospitals or in psychiatric units within a general hospital, many health nuts might not find this to be the ideal setting. Indeed, work in this kind of setting requires a strong spirit. Seeing human suffering like this can be very difficult to deal with on a daily basis. That said, there is a great need for caring individuals who want to help improve the mental health of these patients.

## What the Work Is Like

A typical day in the life of a psychiatric nurse in a hospital begins with reviewing the report from the last shift to find out what was happening on the unit. The nurse greets all the patients he or she is assigned to and discusses with them any special activities for the day, such as meetings with the recreational therapist or occupational therapist. Later in the day the nurse dispenses medications, then talks individually with the patients about why they're in the hospital and how they're feeling.

A psychiatric nurse spends a lot of time setting limits and redirecting or trying to control behavior. Sometimes the behavior turns aggressive or violent, so it helps if the nurses are in good physical shape and able to cope with any unruly behavior.

Hospital counselors also teach patients about their medications and help them look for alternative ways to deal with their problems. Administrative duties are important, charting the patients' medications or attending meetings with the psychiatrists, social workers, and various therapists to discuss care plans.

It can be very emotionally stressful, exciting, and challenging work, depending on how the counselor views the violence and the behavioral problems. It can be difficult work, dealing with other people's problems; counselors must be careful because they may feel emotionally drained after a difficult work cycle, and they reach a point where they lose the energy to deal with their own problems. Work hours are determined by rotating shifts, which may mean working nights, evenings, or days.

In addition, counselors must spend a great deal of time in conference with senior physicians. The counselor might have different ideas about how a patient should be treated and then will have to commit considerable amounts of time trying to reach a particular physician for medication orders or other instructions.

## Working Conditions

Work conditions vary depending upon the setting. Hospital nurses often work erratic hours—holidays, weekends, nights, evenings, and days. Counselors in a clinic setting generally have the benefit of more traditional hours, Monday through Friday, working only an occasional evening or weekend.

Hospital settings more typically follow a medical model, viewing the people they're helping as "patients" who are sick, relying on medication as a large segment of the therapy process. Therapists in clinics view the people they are helping as basically well. Therapy is usually more active, relying on talking, support, and education, working toward specific, achievable goals.

## Getting a Head Start

If you are in high school or college, you can start off by getting involved in any peer counseling programs your school might offer. Later, you can volunteer and then find part-time work in a variety of mental health settings. During this process you will get a feel for what the work is really like, and you will be able to make an informed choice. You will also learn how to assess yourself and to see if you have what it takes. Most mental health counselors have master's degrees or Ph.D.s, so plan for a good education.

## Sports Psychology

Sports psychology is the application of psychological principles to assist athletes, coaches, and anyone else involved in the pursuit of improved physical performance.

In other countries, sports psychology has been used to assist world-class athletes for many years, probably going back to the 1930s. In the United States it was developed in the 1970s, and now our Olympic contestants, as well as other athletes, are trained in the use of psychological principles to improve performance.

**What the Job Is Like.** Sports psychologists mainly see athletes and coaches and sometimes parents who may be having adverse interactions with their children. Athletes can be all ages and come from grammar school, junior high, high school, college, and professional and Olympic athletic arenas.

The level of stress or tension athletes feel can affect their performance, so sports psychologists generally teach athletes to decrease the amount of stress they experience in order to optimize performance. Too much stress virtually assures that athletes won't do as well, so they sometimes need to be encouraged to relax. But athletes also may need to be encouraged to feel excited enough to perform well.

Sports psychologists also assist through the use of imagery— that is, one's own imagination. Through visualizing techniques, athletes can practice performing successfully in their minds, which improves performance. The experience of Vasily Alexiev, a Russian weight lifter, provides a good illustration of how this works. At one point in his training, his coaches told him to do a maneuver with a weight below a weight he had previously been successful with. He complied. They then took him to the scales and showed him that the weight he had lifted was more than a world record and much more than he had ever done before. They tricked him in a very important way, showing him that what he thought had a great impact on what he was capable of doing.

As a sports psychologist, you teach people to imagine things that, if they were true, would produce the desired effect, which increases the probability of achieving the effect. If one were to think of a weight as something other than a weight—something that had to be moved to save a life, for example—you could expect the person to do better using that kind of imagery.

The biathlon, a winter Olympic event in which contestants travel on cross-country skis with a rifle strapped to their backs, provides another good example. After skiing over a long distance of hilly terrain, which is very tiring, the athletes must go immediately to a firing area and shoot the rifle accurately. The problem is that they are out of breath and have rapid heartbeats, which makes it very difficult to hold a rifle steady. Even a heartbeat—if it is, for instance, at 180 beats a minute, which is not uncommon—can cause the barrel of a gun to move. Not very many people can shoot accurately under those circumstances. But knowing the physiological nature of the problem, sports psychologists can teach athletes to reduce their heart rates very quickly with a single thought—similar to the meditative techniques known to yoga adepts.

Richard Suinn, who has been an Olympic psychologist for several years, trained the first American athlete who medaled in the biathlon to change his heart rate from 180 beats per minute down to 80 in a very short period of time. He did this by pairing a word with a relaxed state. When the athlete reached the firing area and said the word to himself, he was able to decrease his heart rate very rapidly. The word was *rock*, but any word can be used—the important thing is that it must become meaningful to the individual.

Sports psychologists work with many athletes in this way, having them imagine perfecting their technical skills and achieving better control of themselves and teaching them healthy ways to think in order to decrease their stress.

Psychologists also teach the principles of learning and motivation to coaches so they can effectively use positive as well as negative reinforcement. They teach coaches to be more sensitive to their players' differing needs. Some young athletes are in the sport for more social reasons, yet they want to improve their skills, while others are involved solely for their competitive needs. People are different, and you might need to motivate them very differently. Some athletes have large egos and don't like criticism, while others can take a whole lot of correction, even in front of other team members, and learn from it. Coaches need to be taught how to be sensitive, to pay close attention to what they observe in each athlete, in order to get the team working at peak performance levels.

Keep in mind that sports psychology is not an office job. Instead, your work is on the field, where you watch and interact with the players. For many this is a benefit to the profession, but it can also be a downside. You might be spending a considerable amount of time in activities for which you're not being paid.

**Getting Started in Sports Psychology.** There are no pure sports psychology training programs; most sports psychologists have Ph.D.s or related degrees in clinical psychology and study sports psychology as a subspecialty. Some psychologists make sports psychology the focus of their practice; others incorporate the principles and techniques into a general practice.

But getting into a clinical psychology program is very competitive. There are hundreds of applications for each opening. Applicants must have good grades and do well on their GREs.

The doctoral program is generally four to five years above the bachelor's, and then to be licensed, most states require you to pass a written and oral examination and have completed fifteen hundred hours of postdoctoral supervised training.

## What Makes a Good Counselor

Counselors need to possess certain skills. How many can you check off?

__ Good people skills/ability to interact well with people
__ Ability to be supportive and nurturing
__ Good listening skills
__ Flexible attitude
__ Tolerance toward people you don't understand
__ Well organized

**Test Your Self-Esteem.** Counselors regularly work with clients and patients who suffer from low self-esteem, but before these professionals can be really effective, they must have a strong sense of their own self-worth.

How high is your self-esteem? Answer the statements *True* or *False*, then find your rating.

1. I normally feel warm and happy toward myself.
2. I normally speak up for my own opinions.
3. I normally do my own thinking and make my own decisions.
4. I willingly take responsibility for the consequences of my actions.
5. I feel free to express love, anger, joy, resentment, and all my other emotions.
6. I rarely experience jealousy, envy, or suspicion.
7. I don't feel put down or rejected if someone disagrees with me.
8. I readily admit my mistakes, shortcomings, and defeats.
9. I can make and keep friends without exerting myself.

10. Everything doesn't always have to be perfect.
11. I accept compliments and gifts without embarrassment.
12. I am normally friendly, considerate, and generous with others.

The more questions you were able to answer with *True*, the better your self-esteem. Count your *True* answers, then find your score below.

0 to 4 — You need to work on your self-esteem. Talk to someone you trust about the things that concern you.

5 to 8 — Your self-esteem is not too bad, but there are still areas you could work on. Again, discuss your concerns with a counselor or someone else whose opinion you respect.

9 to 12 — Congratulations! Your self-esteem is excellent. You are confident and mature and you really take care of yourself. You'd make a great counselor.

# CHAPTER THREE

# Healing with Plants

For thousands of years people have recognized the healing properties of plants. Before the creation of synthetic medicines, ancient cultures were knowledgeable about each plant's function and how to tap into its strengths. In addition to their aesthetic value and their life-sustaining importance as food, plants have always been the basis for curing common and not-so-common ailments.

In modern times in the United States, this discipline has become almost a lost art. But not quite. Health nuts around the world still recognize the value of plants for healing. Dr. Andrew Weil and other authors have helped to popularize herbal therapies. Health nuts who also love plants can find rewarding careers in this area.

## Herbalism

The old Webster's dictionary from the 1800s defined an herbalist as one involved with the commerce of plants: an herb doctor or root doctor. Today, most people refer to herbalists as those who use or pick herbs for medicine. Professional herbalists fall into several different categories.

- **Wildcrafters** pick herbs that are going to be used for medicinal purposes.
- **Farmers** who specifically grow herbs for medicine are considered to be herbalists.
- **Herbologists** study and identify herbs but don't necessarily use them.

Many herbalists, through writing and lecturing, are involved in teaching people the medicinal value of plants. They may write books and magazine articles and teach classes across the country. They may consult with people about their health needs and which types of herbs they can use to deal with different types of ailments. Some work full-time for manufacturers of medicinal products and may be responsible for quality control and answering customers' questions.

Many different cultures have rich traditions of using herbs in maintaining health and healing sick individuals. Native Americans have traditionally possessed a wealth of knowledge about using herbs. When people got sick, the medicine people picked herbs and made teas or poultices. While many Native Americans incorporate Western healing practices into their general health care, the use of healing herbs continues to be practiced.

In fact, around the United States, herbs are used to maintain health across cultures. Caribbean ethnobotany (local cultural use of plants for medicine) features a variety of herb doctors who diagnose and treat ailments. Traditional Chinese medicine is another field that has been practiced for thousands of years and is growing in acceptance and respect in Western cultures.

Although herbalism has been practiced pretty much in the same manner for thousands of years, finding true recognition through established health-industry channels in this country could take another millennium or two, American herbalists believe.

## What the Work Is Like

Herbalists are familiar with the medicinal properties of various herbs and know which herbs can help with particular physical or emotional problems. However, unless licensed as either a naturopathic doctor or an acupuncturist, they cannot set up an office and practice medicine in this country, even if in that practice all they are doing is recommending herbal teas. This is because the FDA regulates dispensation of substances for medicinal use. Neither herbalists nor anyone else can legally dispense a substance for medicinal use unless that substance has been approved by the FDA. If you give garlic to someone, for example, and tell him or her that it can help lower cholesterol levels—which has been documented in some medical studies—you can be arrested for dispensing illicit drugs. Therefore, herbalists work to improve research on plant-based medicines and gain acceptance in the mainstream of U.S. health care.

If you have walked into any nutrition or health-food store and seen the rows of bottles and vials holding all the different herbs in their various forms, you may be thinking, "Wait a minute, those are medicinal, aren't they?" In essence, those nonapproved substances might be considered illegal. How do manufacturers and retailers buck the system? The answer is simple. The products are not packaged as medicines; they are called "foods." (You can read more about careers in natural food stores in Chapter 5.)

Trained herbalists know what to do with these "foods." They are aware of how the popular medications used in this country— aspirins and sedatives, for example—can be replaced safely with common plants. Aspirin was originally derived from a plant called meadowsweet. The Latin name at that time was spirea, which is where the 'spir' in 'aspirin' came from. So, if someone has a headache, for example, an herbalist would use a natural source, such as a tea made with meadowsweet.

There are more than a million prescriptions written for the sedative Valium every year, which involves a $65 doctor visit, a $30 prescription, and possible side effects from the drug. Herbalists would treat the same ailment with something as simple as chamomile tea. Chamomile is a flower with essential oils that have sedative properties. There is a whole range of calming herbs that get progressively stronger—from chamomile to skullcap to valerian root.

Herbalists promote the use of herbs in healing without resorting to breaking the law. They teach and write books and articles, they lecture and offer apprentice programs, or they work for herbal product manufacturers.

## Jobs with Herbal Product Manufacturers

There are several job positions available within the herbal product manufacturing industry for those interested in how herbs can be used, marketed, and manufactured. These include:

- **Research and development** of products, developing formulas and processing techniques
- **Quality control**, ensuring that the plants being used are the right plants, that they are not contaminated, and that they have the appropriate potency
- **Writing literature** to describe the products
- **Teaching classes** to increase consumer awareness about the different products

## Training

For those seeking training as herbalists, there are a number of residency programs in the United States. There are also correspondence courses and various lectures, seminars, and workshops held across the country. The American Herbalist Guild publishes an inexpensive directory that lists all the different programs. It is available by writing to them at the address listed in Appendix A.

Presently, there are only two mechanisms by which someone can be licensed to practice medicine and utilize herbs in his or her practice. The first is to become licensed as a naturopathic physician. Naturopathic physicians are fully trained through medical schools and are called N.D.s, as opposed to M.D.s. Naturopathic medicine uses the principles of nature, such as nutrition, exercise, herbal medicine, and other preventative and holistic approaches, to encourage and sustain health.

The second way to become licensed to use herbs is as an acupuncturist. Acupuncture is a foundation of Chinese medicine, and herbalism plays a large role in that discipline. Some acupuncture schools emphasize herbal medicine more than others.

# Pharmacognosy

Pharmacognosy is the study of the medicinal actions of plants and other natural products. It doesn't cover, as herbalism does, the practice of herbal medicine or the picking of medicinal plants. The related discipline, pharmacology, is the study of the medicinal actions of substances in general.

It is the job of pharmacognosy professionals to pick the plant apart and study its constituents. Some Native American herbalists, for example, might not know that a plant contains volatile oils, alkaloids, and polysaccharides, but they know how to use it and how it works in the body. The well-known Dr. Andrew Weil, for example, devoted much of his early career to assimilating the plant knowledge of native medicine men or shamans throughout the Americas.

In contrast, a pharmacognosist studies the plant constituents scientifically but wouldn't necessarily know how to use the plants. The end result of their study is to develop synthetic drugs from natural substances.

At one time, physicians were trained in botany because they needed to know where their medicines came from. But then there was a separation between pharmacy and medicine, and other sub-specialties were created, such as pharmacology and pharmacognosy, which continued the study of medicinal plants. Like herbalism, pharmacognosy became an endangered species, but within the past thirty years, both disciplines have enjoyed a resurgence. Today, the University of Illinois has one of the most widely recognized training programs in the country in pharmacognosy.

# Horticultural Therapy

Any health nut who loves plants can tell you that being close to the soil—working with plants or just sitting in a fragrant and colorful garden—has therapeutic value. Horticultural activity has long been known to relieve tension, improve physical condition, and promote a sense of accomplishment, pride, and well-being.

The earliest physicians in ancient Egypt prescribed walks in the garden for their mentally ill patients. The early American physician Benjamin Rush, who signed the Declaration of Independence, encouraged his psychiatric patients to tend gardens. In 1879, Pennsylvania's Friends Asylum for the Insane (today renamed Friends Hospital) built the first known greenhouse for use with mentally ill patients. And after World War II, veterans hospitals—with the help of scores of garden club volunteers—also promoted similar activity for their patients.

Today, horticultural therapy is an emerging science based on this time-tested art. In 1955, Michigan State University awarded the first undergraduate degree in horticultural therapy, and in 1971, Kansas State University established the first graduate program in the field.

## What a Horticultural Therapist Does

Horticultural therapists use activities involving plants and other natural materials to improve a person's social, educational, psychological, or physical adjustment. Therapists work with people who are physically or developmentally disabled, the elderly, drug and alcohol abusers, prisoners, and those who are socially or economically disadvantaged.

The thinking behind horticultural therapy is that plants possess life-enhancing qualities that people respond to. In a judgmental world, plants are nonthreatening and nondiscriminating. Plants are living entities that respond directly to the care that is given them. In short, they provide a benevolent setting in which a person can take the first steps toward mental and physical healing.

Horticultural therapists, in addition to utilizing standard gardening routines, also introduce alternative methods that are sensitive to the special needs of patients. This involves building wide paths and gently graded entrances and constructing raised beds to make gardening accessible to wheelchairs. Tools are also adapted, such as short handles for wheelchair-bound individuals and long handles for those with weak backs.

## Finding That Job

Because of the continued growth of horticultural therapy, the demand for trained therapists has continued to rise. Horticultural therapists find work in rehab hospitals, nursing homes, substance-abuse treatment centers, prisons, botanical gardens, and inner-city programs. Online research is an invaluable way to locate jobs and research companies. For example, Kansas State University in Manhattan, Kansas, maintains a job bank online (www.ksu.edu), and the American Horticultural Therapy Association (AHTA) lists openings its members post (www.ahta.org). Some positions find their way into the help-wanted section of local newspapers, but most horticultural therapists learn about positions through word of mouth—or they create their own jobs.

Often, administrators of rehab centers, hospitals, and other appropriate settings aren't aware of the benefits of a horticultural therapy program. Enterprising therapists with PR skills have learned how to convince administrators that their services are needed. Many begin by volunteering, working with patients or clients at the hospitals or through a local botanical garden.

## Training

Because horticultural therapy is such a young discipline, finding training is not an easy process. Currently, Kansas State University's Department of Horticulture, Forestry, and Recreation Resources is the best known of a few colleges and universities that offer bachelor's and master's degree programs in horticultural therapy in the United States. However, many more schools (program addresses can be found in Appendix B) offer bachelor's degrees in horticulture with course options in horticultural therapy. Edmonds Community College in Lynnwood, Washington, awards a two-year associate's degree in horticultural therapy, and various other institutions, such as Massachusetts Bay Community College and Temple University, offer horticultural therapy electives. Certificate programs and stand-alone courses are widely available. An aspiring horticultural therapist can take several routes to become qualified. Horticulture involves the art and science of growing and culturing plant material in intensive or adapted environments. To work effectively with people, the student must also be well trained in psychology, sociology, and education. Architectural knowledge is also helpful in creating accessible landscapes. Students can pursue a number of other areas, such as speech pathology, communications, computer science, robotics, and human anatomy and muscle movement. Students in Kansas State's program spend a six-month internship gaining practical on-the-job training. They are supervised by registered horticultural therapists in established programs and are placed coast to coast, from Friends Hospital in Philadelphia to the Chicago Botanical Gardens.

A four-year degree, although desirable, is not necessary to find work as a horticultural therapist because there are different levels of entry into the field. In this country, many volunteers belong to garden clubs and master gardener groups taught by the Cooperative Extension Service. There are some programs that train at the associate arts level for people who don't have the extra time to devote to their training, but in the future the entry for many areas of employment in horticultural therapy will most likely be at the graduate level.

Multidiscipline training will help you apply what's best known in all the related fields and will make you more desirable to future employers. A good example is the importance of business and marketing skills. Many horticultural therapy programs today are cost-effective; that is, they are self-sufficient. But in order to utilize the valuable products being produced—whether sacks of potatoes from a vegetable garden or flowers or a landscaping service being provided—you also need some kind of skills in how to market the product.

Although not every employer of horticultural therapists requires registration, being a registered therapist greatly increases your chances of landing a good job. Registration provides recognition as an accomplished therapist who has received the established training and helps to keep the profession's standards high. Becoming a registered horticultural therapist does not require a degree in horticultural therapy. A degree in a related field or a combination of work experience and education can all lead to professional registration. There are three levels of registration:

- **Horticultural Therapy Technician or Assistant (H.T.T./ H.T.A.).** This is the designation for the technician who has generally gone through a two-year certification program.
- **Horticultural Therapist, Registered (H.T.R.).** This designation is for someone who holds a bachelor's degree.
- **Master Horticultural Therapist (H.T.M.).** This is for the person with a graduate degree and several years' experience.

Decisions about registration are peer-reviewed by a committee from the American Horticultural Therapy Association. The committee members follow a point system, awarding points for the number of years of experience, for publications, for attending seminars, for the number and type of degrees earned, and for other related activities.

## Salaries

The American Horticultural Therapy Association conducts an annual survey to determine salary levels for nonregistered therapists, H.T.T.s, H.T.R.s, and H.T.M.s. The results of the most recent poll (mid-1990s) show that the average salary of therapists with one year or less of employment experience is $24,920 per year. Averages go up with the number of years of working experience. Therapists can expect to make an average of $26,756 with one to five years of experience, $27,263 with five to ten years of experience, and $33,070 with ten or more years' experience.

Salaries increase by $1,500 to approximately $2,500 per year of additional work experience for those who have obtained professional registration. Contact the American Horticultural Therapy Association for results of a 2003 salary study that is under way as this book goes to press.

Sometimes part-time jobs are available at an hourly wage. For example, in 2002 a job combining horticultural therapy with music therapy at an Atlanta-area hospital was advertise at a rate of $15 per hour.

# CHAPTER FOUR

# Let's Get Physical

Physical fitness is important to most health nuts. In addition to carefully monitoring what food they eat, fitness-minded health nuts make time for regular exercise. They walk, jog, take aerobics classes, ride bicycles, participate in sports, or work out at health clubs or gyms.

For health nuts with athletic ability, what could be more ideal than to incorporate their love of physical fitness into a rewarding career? As trainers, instructors, coaches, and recreation workers, these skilled athletic types organize and lead programs and watch over recreational facilities and equipment. They help people to pursue their interests in sports or body building for the purpose of entertainment, physical fitness, or self-improvement. As physical, occupational, or recreational therapists, they help people with physical limitations reach their full potential. As you can see from the chart below, fitness buffs of all types are employed in a variety of settings, and the numbers look promising!

**TABLE 4.1.** Fitness and Health Industry, 2001–2002

|  | U.S. TOTALS |
| --- | --- |
| Number of health clubs | 17,807 |
| Number of health club members | 33.8 million |
| Industry revenue | $12.2 billion |
| Industry payroll | $5.1 billion |
| Full-time employees | 160,000 |
| Part-time employees | 635,000 |

Source: International Health, Racquet & Sportsclub Association (IHRSA).

## Sports and Recreation Professionals

The term *recreation worker* encompasses a variety of jobs. Rec workers may do anything from coaching sports to teaching arts and crafts. Basically, recreation is anything people do for fun. Many communities in the United States organize such activities and hire full-time staffers who must work while their clients engage in leisure activities. Depending upon the setting, the majority of workers put in a forty-hour week, but many of those hours can be spent in the evenings or on weekends. Jobs can also be seasonal, such as at summer camps or with certain sports.

### Job Settings

Athletic health nuts can find full- and part-time work in a variety of settings. And while with some jobs relocation is a must to further a career, physical fitness experts need only take a walk through the neighborhood or scan the Yellow Pages to find employment close to home.

The following is a list of possible job settings. You can read more about each setting throughout this chapter.

- Cruise ships
- Health clubs, spas, and gyms
- Adult education programs
- Parks and recreation departments
- National Park Service (Read more about National Park Service careers in Chapter 7.)
- Summer camps
- YMCA, Boy Scouts, Red Cross
- Schools, colleges, and universities
- Hospitals
- Nursing homes
- Rehab centers
- Clinics

## Training and Qualifications

The training and qualifications required for the different recreation fields could range from a high school diploma (or less for some summer camp jobs) to a bachelor's or master's degree for supervisory or management positions and those positions that require more extensive training and education.

A background in a specialty, such as athletics or karate, is usually a must. Some jobs also require special certificates, such as lifesaving certification for water-related activities or teacher's certification for physical education instructors working in the public school system.

Various associate's and bachelor's degree programs are offered throughout the country in parks and recreation, leisure studies, fitness management, and related disciplines.

The ideal recreation worker should be outgoing, creative, good at motivating people, and sensitive to the needs of others. Good health and physical fitness, needless to say, are also required.

# Cruise Ship Careers

Probably everyone, at one time or another, has seen television reruns of "The Love Boat" and watched Julie, Doc, Issac, Gopher, and Captain Steubing go about their daily activities, interacting with passengers while ensuring that they have the best vacations of their lives. Although reality might not exactly mirror life on the popular series, being part of a cruise ship staff can be fun and exciting, with the opportunity to travel to exotic ports, meet all different kinds of people, and lead a carefree lifestyle. In the close quarters of a ship, the people you work with become like a family. Sometimes you have to share a cabin with another crew member and you strike up new friendships as a result.

Job titles and responsibilities vary from ship to ship. For example, the term *cruise staff* is often synonymous with assistant cruise director or social or activities director.

Although filled with its share of excitement and glamour, working on a ship involves a lot of hard work. Cruise staff put in long hours—anywhere from eight to fifteen hours a day, seven days a week—and must maintain a high level of energy and always be cordial and friendly to passengers, even when you don't feel like it. You may have to be on the sports deck by 9 A.M., down in the lounge by 9:30, getting ready in your cabin to be back up on the deck by 10, and so on. Staff are on a rigid time schedule.

Cruise staff members are generally in charge of organizing activities and social events, including classic shipboard games such as shuffleboard and ring toss, bingo, aerobics classes, basketball, golf putting (and driving—off the stern of the ship), rock climbing, in-line skating, yoga, and pool games. Some cruises cater to those who prefer "extreme" sports activities, such as windsurfing and jet skiing, and some ships have added facilities, such as rock-climbing walls. Sports and fitness theme cruises are available widely. Activities directors also socialize at cocktail parties and masquerade balls and take every opportunity to make sure passengers feel comfortable and are enjoying themselves.

In a way, being a cruise staff member is similar to being a camp counselor, but for adults. Staff must make sure the passengers are having fun, and they work hard to come up with activities and events to capture their interest. They might organize a tea, give an origami (paper folding) demonstration, or stage a treasure hunt. When in port, they each chaperone a group of passengers on a tour. Even between scheduled activities, they constantly interact and socialize with the passengers.

When in port, most of the crew members have time off to go ashore and explore, since there are no days off while at sea. Activities aboard ship usually follow a rigid schedule, with little time in between for the crew to rest and take a break. Cruise staff move quickly from one activity to another, announcing games over the loudspeaker, setting up the deck for exercise classes, supervising ring-toss tournaments or other special events, and encouraging everyone to participate.

An outgoing, energetic individual would be in his or her element in such a job; someone who lacks those traits might find the work very difficult.

## Salaries

While salaries are not overly generous, the additional benefits are. Cruise staff are provided with free housing and all they can eat while on board ship. It's not necessary for a full-time employee of a cruise line to maintain quarters ashore; therefore, most of the salary can be saved.

Cruise ships also sail to exotic ports, giving staff members the chance to travel and meet people from all over the world.

## Training

A college education is not necessary for these types of positions, but some cruise lines prefer to see an applicant with a degree in psychology, hotel management, physical education, or communications. It's also a good idea to know another language, especially Spanish or German.

Even more important are the following personal qualities a good cruise staff member should possess:

- Patience
- Diplomacy
- Tolerance for a wide variety of people
- A never-ending supply of energy
- An outgoing and genuinely friendly nature
- Enthusiasm
- Artistic talent
- Athletic ability

Most successful applicants land their jobs by applying directly to the various cruise lines, which are located mainly in Miami, Fort Lauderdale, Los Angeles, San Francisco, and New York. Look through the Yellow Pages in each city for cruise line addresses and phone numbers or consult *How to Get a Job with a Cruise Line,* listed in Appendix C.

## Fitness Trainers in Health Clubs, Spas, and Gyms

Health clubs, spas, and gyms offer employment to a large number of qualified health nuts. Job titles include the following:

- Personal trainer
- Fitness instructor
- Aerobics instructor
- Racquetball/squash instructor
- Masseur/masseuse
- Nutritionist (see Chapter 5)

To meet safety standards and insurance and state and local regulations, most health clubs require that their instructors and trainers have appropriate qualifications or licenses. And because the field of fitness is constantly evolving—from all the latest fitness fads to new research about how to achieve and maintain health—you have to stay on top of the latest health news to be the best trainer. You also need an upbeat and enthusiastic attitude, and you have to practice what you preach. Clients are more likely to follow the instruction of someone who has achieved the results they're looking for.

Caring is also important. You need to have a firm hand but also possess diplomatic skills. Many of the professionals in this setting hold a great deal of responsibility for their clients' welfare and must be fully trained in what they do.

### What the Job Is Like

Being a fitness instructor involves checking the equipment before the client actually uses it and knowing the best ways to use it to achieve maximum results without injury. You have to be fully aware of the human body and how it should and shouldn't move. If there are any complications or special populations you're working with—for example, diabetics, cardiac rehab patients, arthritis sufferers, or pregnant women—there will be different ways to train them and you'll have to be aware that not everybody can be exercised in the same manner.

There are a variety of settings in which a fitness instructor can work. One of the benefits of working in a health club is that you won't have to generate business—the clients are already there in the club. Or, you can set up a private practice as a personal fitness trainer either at your own place or by visiting a client's home. Keep in mind that once you're outside the club setting, an entirely different insurance coverage is required. If you work out of your own home or in a client's home, you need to protect yourself, both legally and with insurance. At a club, you are covered under the club's insurance. No matter what the setting, safety is key.

As a certified personal trainer, you work extensively with nutrition and kinesiology, which is the study of the movement of the body and how the muscles react to certain exercises. You must also know first aid. All personal trainers must be certified in CPR.

While working with people who want to improve their fitness, you first have to take a health history, which involves asking a series of questions—including age, whether or not they smoke, and whether there is a family history of health risk factors. If a person doesn't appear to be able to jump into a fitness routine, you may have to refer him or her to a physician before beginning any exercise program. Such a person may be a forty-five-year-old male who smokes, is overweight, and has had somebody in his family with diabetes. It is the physician's job and not yours to do a stress test and see if the client is ready. Trainers are not qualified to diagnose ailments; they can only refer the individual to an M.D. and await the results before beginning a training regimen based on the physician's report.

If the client is ready to begin the exercise program, the trainer will make a personal fitness assessment. The training program must work in all the elements of physical fitness, such as flexibility, muscular strength and endurance, cardiovascular endurance, and body composition. Normally a training session is an hour or two maximum, and clients may come once or twice a week to meet with the trainer in addition to their self-directed workouts on the off days.

## Salaries

Personal trainers in a health club can work on commission or for an hourly rate, earning as much as $45 to $150 an hour, depending upon the clientele. The general run of salaries for fitness trainers is more modest. A range of $7.65 to $17 per hour is typical for most, with $10.96 as a national median. The top 10 percent earns $25 and up. See Table 4.2 for a breakdown of the financial compensation among fitness professionals.

One of the major nonmonetary benefits of this work is that you can set your own hours, part-time or full-time, and make adjustments depending on your lifestyle. Keep in mind that, if you're self-employed, you must factor in taxes and insurance expenses.

## Training

Several different routes provide future trainers with the knowledge of their craft and certification. Universities offer four-year

---

**TABLE 4.2. Hourly Wages for Fitness Trainers**

| JOB TITLE | AVERAGE HOURLY WAGE |
| --- | --- |
| Fitness trainers/aerobic instructors | $10.96 (median) |
| Top 10 percent of trainers/instructors | $25.98 or more |
| Trainers in commercial fitness clubs | $12.22 |
| Trainers in civic associations | $9.06 |

*Source: U.S. Bureau of Labor Statistics, Occupational Outlook Handbook.*

majors and even graduate programs in exercise science or exercise physiology. Another route is a home-study course through the American Council on Exercise (ACE), followed by a formal exam, given four times a year. The American College of Sports Medicine (ACSM) is also a certifying body. Both organizations require tests with written and/or practical components.

The ACSM requires candidates to demonstrate knowledge, skills, and abilities vital to the profession. Its test has both a written, multiple-choice format and a practical examination component wherein candidates demonstrate safe and correct fitness assessment techniques and skills.

The ACSM practical examination covers three areas: body composition, with flexibility and strength; a strength and conditioning exercise demonstration; and a cardiovascular fitness assessment. The practical examination is administered at a nationwide network of host sites supervised by ACSM. All use the same objective scoring method. The practical test consists of sub-max testing, in which you are evaluated while you monitor a client's heart rate and blood pressure. You will also put your client through a workout, and your spotting techniques and how you interact will be judged.

For those personal trainers who have already established themselves in business, ASCM provides continuing education options. Participants take eighty continuing education credits during a four-year period. A training program can take two weeks, eight weeks, or as long as four years, if the goal is a bachelor's degree.

For more information on training and certification, you can contact ACE and ACSM, which are both listed in Appendix A.

· · · · · · · · · · · · · · · · · · · · · · · · · · · · · · ·

## Fitness Instrutors

There are many community-based areas in which a fitness instructor can find work, no matter how large or small the community. These include adult education programs, parks and recreation departments, organizations such as the YMCA or the Boy

Scouts, summer camps, and educational institutions from elementary schools to universities.

## Adult Education Programs

Most communities offer health and fitness programs as part of a regular series of adult education or continuing education classes, usually held in the evenings at local schools or at adult education facilities, where classes can be offered during the day as well.

Depending upon their specialty, some instructors need to apply for certification through the state school board. In that case, most program directors walk their job applicants through the process. Other specialties require only that you demonstrate some expertise and an ability to instruct.

A look through the adult education class listings in your community will give you an idea where you might be able to fit in. Some courses regularly offered that would appeal to health nuts include:

- Aerobics
- Boating safety
- Dance (anything from line dancing to folk dancing, ballet, or ballroom dancing)
- Gymnastics
- Karate
- Sailing
- Scuba diving
- Weight training
- Yoga

Pay is usually hourly and based on your education and experience. Although for the most part this field offers only part-time employment, teaching an adult education class is a way for health nuts to share their knowledge, stay fit, and earn extra income at the same time.

## Parks and Recreation Departments

Most cities have parks and recreation departments through which various activities are offered to the public at little or no cost. Many of the same classes offered through adult education are offered here as well, providing instructors and coaches with additional opportunities for employment.

In addition to a wide variety of sports—from tennis and football to volleyball and soccer—many Little League teams originate through community parks and recreation departments.

## The YMCA, the Boy and Girl Scouts, and the Red Cross

These and similar enterprises provide recreation and sports activities for children and adults. Recreation workers and instructors can find work based at their town facilities or at day camps and resident camps located in country settings. Often, these organizations sponsor summer camp programs in addition to regular classes.

## Summer Camps

Camp counselors lead children and teenage campers in outdoor-oriented forms of recreation, such as swimming, hiking, and horseback riding. Counselors also provide campers with specialized instruction in activities such as archery, boating, gymnastics, and tennis. At overnight camps, counselors are also responsible for supervising daily living tasks and general socialization.

The pay is usually low, but free room and board are always provided. Camp counseling is an excellent opportunity for college students to gain skills and earn extra money during their summer vacations.

## Schools, Colleges, and Universities

Most educational institutions require students to participate in some form of physical education, whether individual activities, such as swimming or gymnastics, or team sports, such as basketball or football. Opportunities therefore exist for physical education teachers and athletic coaches.

Within primary and secondary education, physical education teachers are required to have at least a bachelor's degree and a teaching certificate issued by the state. Athletic coaches usually are required to teach another subject—English, math, or science, for example—in addition to their coaching duties.

At the college level, physical education teachers are usually required to have master's or doctoral degrees. Coaches who have a good track record of successful wins are generally sought out.

Other careers for sports-minded people include sports medicine and sports psychology, highlighted in Chapter 2.

## Physical Therapists

Although many health nuts prefer to work with a well population, there are also many who derive great satisfaction from helping those with physical or emotional limitations. The purpose of physical therapy is to correct muscular-skeletal dysfunction and problems with movement. The physical therapist works independently, evaluating patients and designing and implementing treatment plans.

Physical therapists work with a variety of patients or problems:

- Premature infants
- Pediatric patients
- Obstetric patients
- People with sports or traumatic injuries
- People with birth or genetic defects
- People with back or neck injuries
- Stroke victims
- Burn and wound victims
- Amputees
- Dancers and performing artists

- Athletes
- People with multiple sclerosis, Parkinson's disease, or neurological injuries
- Post-op patients
- Geriatric patients

The role of the physical therapist is becoming very specialized. Physical therapists tend to work in a particular setting or with certain kinds of patients. They evaluate patients, looking for pain, flexibility or range of motion, strength, and what kinds of functional activities patients do or need to do. For example, a dancer needs to dance, a child needs to play, and so on, so the physical therapist's job is to help the patient achieve the ability to accomplish these activities. A complete evaluation involves meeting with the patient, discussing his or her concerns and maladies, then designing an appropriate treatment plan.

Treatment plans generally include manual therapy, stretching or strengthening exercises, or specific joint mobilization exercises. Therapists may use modalities such as hot packs, cold packs, ultrasound, or electric stimulation to help reduce pain.

They are involved in teaching, too, explaining the exercises to the patients so they can carry on the activities at home on their own. If the patients are children, the therapist also works with the child's parents or teachers. On the sports field a therapist may be educating the coaches about what kinds of exercises a specific child needs.

A therapist also teaches classes on topics such as the back, body awareness, or risk management. Classes may be offered within a hospital, in the community, at workplaces, and so forth.

A necessary part of the job is thorough paperwork documentation—that's the part most therapists don't like, but it's necessary.

## Job Settings

While those not in the know might think of physical therapists as working only in hospital settings, in actuality, there is a wide range of settings open to physical therapy professionals. In addition to seeing patients in acute-care hospitals, both inpatient and outpatient, physical therapists see patients in their homes, providing home health care; in schools, working with students on the playing fields; in nursing homes; in rehab hospitals; in private practices; and in industry, doing job-site analyses that help prevent injuries. As an example, a large corporation could hire a physical therapist to evaluate risks the employees encounter, then, by taking the therapist's recommendations, could redesign the workplace and lower the number of worker compensation claims.

Physical therapists can also work for a traveling company. This kind of company makes sure that you are licensed in the state you are sent to on assignment, moving whenever and wherever there is a need.

## Training

Physical therapists must have at least a bachelor's degree. Some go on for a master's degree, and others earn a doctorate. Most schools require anywhere from twenty to one hundred hours of observation time before future P.T.s can even apply to be admitted to a program. This observation time can be clocked while volunteering or working as a physical therapy aide, an on-the-job training position explained later in this chapter. Physical therapy programs can be found through the American Physical Therapy Association, listed in Appendix A.

Course work covers mostly math and sciences as well as specific training in the techniques used in physical therapy, including exercise science and exercise physiology. Although the training is similar to that undertaken by personal trainers, physical therapy training is more medically based. Physical therapy students study more pathology, doing cadaver dissections, for example. The study of anatomy and physiology is more extensive, as is muscle pathology. But the differences are explained easily by the different people each works with. Personal trainers deal with a healthy population for the most part; physical therapists work with patients who have disabilities or a variety of other physical problems.

There are several levels of employment within the field of physical therapy. Here are a few job titles and descriptions.

**Physical Therapist Assistant.** While the physical therapist is responsible for the design of treatment plans, the physical therapist assistant is trained to carry out those plans. Limitations for physical therapist assistants are that they cannot update or change treatment plans.

Training for a physical therapist assistant career involves a two-year program ending with an associate's degree.

**Physical Therapy Aide.** Physical therapy aides are usually trained on the job. They can't do direct patient care, but they help both the physical therapist and the physical therapist assistant. Aides might help a patient count the number of exercises he or she is doing, move equipment, bring patients to the treatment areas, or help a person walk or transfer from the bed to a chair.

**Assistant Director.** An assistant director supervises all physical therapy in a hospital and may also be responsible for hiring and working with the P.T.s to develop their skills. Administrative personnel at the assistant director level are also responsible for developing and following the budget, including balancing the expenses and ordering equipment.

## Salaries

As a newly graduated physical therapist, you can make an excellent starting salary—between $35,000 to $40,000 a year, depending upon the region of the country in which you practice. In the year 2000, according to the Bureau of Labor Statistics, the lowest 10 percent of salaries were in the range of $38,500, while the median salary per year was $54,800. Salaries increase with the number of years' experience. (See Table 4.3.)

Physical therapists working in home health can make $40 to $50 an hour, and nationwide statistics for 2000 set median salaries for home health P.T.s at $57,830 a year. The median annual earnings of physical therapists in doctor's offices and clinics was $58,390 in the year 2000. Physical therapists in private practice can make between $85,000 and $100,000 a year, but self-employed physical therapists have more expenses to cover, too, such as liability insurance. In private practice, a physical therapist has to wear many hats, one of which is that of bill collector. And it can be difficult sometimes to collect payments. Traveling physical therapists usually make a good hourly wage and have all expenses covered, including flights, rental cars, hotel rooms, and meals.

In 2000, the beginning assistant brought home $19,670, according to a survey by the American Physical Therapy Association. Physical therapy assistants with two-year degrees can start earning between $20,000 and $30,000 a year.

The nonprofessional position of physical therapy aide typically earns minimum wage.

**TABLE 4.3. Salaries for Physical Therapists**

| JOB TITLE | MEDIAN SALARY |
|---|---|
| **Physical Therapists** | |
| I to 3 years' experience | $43,000 |
| 4 to 6 years' experience | $50,000 |
| 7 to 9 years' experience | $55,000 |
| 10 to 15 years' experience | $60,000 |
| | |
| **Physical Therapy Aides/Assistants** | |
| Assistants | $33,870 |
| Aides | $19,670 |

Source: 2001 Practice Profile, American Physical Therapy Association, and the U.S. Department of Labor, Bureau of Labor Statistics, Occupational Outlook Handbook.

## Job Outlook

The job outlook for physical therapists is excellent. It's predicted that job growth will be much faster than average for this field through 2010. A shortage of physical therapists exists for two main reasons. First, capabilities and problems that the physical therapist is qualified to handle have expanded, creating more of a demand. Second, because academia doesn't pay well, there is a shortage of qualified people willing to teach in physical therapy training programs. When the teacher makes less money than the student, there is little motivation to follow that career path. Doctorates are required to teach master's and doctoral-level students. The number of qualified teachers is very low, and most physical therapists prefer to work in the field rather than in a classroom. With fewer teachers, fewer physical therapists can be trained, thus contributing to the shortage and increasing the demand.

............................................

# Occupational Therapists

According to the American Occupational Therapy Association, occupational therapy is "a health and rehabilitation profession. Its practitioners provide services to individuals of all ages who have physical, developmental, emotional, and social deficits, and because of these conditions, need specialized assistance in learning skills to enable them to lead independent, productive, and satisfying lives." In essence, occupational therapy is a health profession that helps people do things for themselves within the limits of their disability or disease.

How do occupational therapists do that? They evaluate the patients to see what their skills are or where they have some problems—what the therapists call deficits. Then they have to determine whether they can improve those deficits. For instance, if someone has had a stroke, and he or she has a weak arm on the side of the stroke, the therapist asks whether, through exercise and other activities, the patient can improve the use of the arm so that it will function as well as it did prior to the stroke.

Occupational therapists work with patients to determine whether they have the motor ability, the muscle power, and the strength to perform specific activities. Do they have the necessary coordination? Sometimes they might have the motor power but they lack the dexterity to pick up a coin from the table. That means they would be limited in the tasks they could do for themselves when they returned to daily living.

Sometimes in the patient evaluation, a therapist realizes that an arthritic patient, for example, has lost the ability to manipulate small buttons. Knowing that, therapist and patient together can look into some adaptive equipment such as button hooks, dressing sticks, or elastic shoelaces, which don't need as fine a motor ability to use.

After the assessment, the therapist sets realistic goals with the patient and asks questions such as the following: Where do you want to be functioning in a month? Where do you want to be functioning in three or four months? The goals may be as simple as putting on socks or a sweater or as long-range as being able to sew or play the piano.

Once the patient's goals are established, the therarapist uses various activities to work toward those goals, from putting round pegs in round holes to practicing the piano or using a computer keyboard, depending on what skills they're trying to develop.

Occupational therapists gather baseline data at the start of treatment—they may have initially measured grip and pinch strength—and then, after thirty days, they repeat the measurements to see if there's been improvement. If the goals haven't been reached, they analyze why. It may be that the patient had another stroke or something else interfered. If the goals are met, they make new short-term goals until the patient has reached his or her maximum potential.

## Occupational Versus Physical Therapy

Occupational therapists differ from physical therapists in several ways. Although they have the same goals—to make the patient as independent as possible—physical therapists deal with only the patients' physical difficulties. Occupational therapists work with physical and psychosocial issues. Many occupational therapists work in psychiatric facilities, helping patients to cope with their emotional problems. And some patients have a combination of problems. They might have had a stroke, but they may be suffering from depression as well.

While both types of therapists deal with physical problems, they don't do it in quite the same way. An occupational therapist probably wouldn't help a person with ambulation skills, such as learning how to walk. However, both the physical and occupational therapist might focus on transfer skills, such as helping a person get from the bed to a chair, from the chair to a standing position.

## Job Settings

Occupational therapists work with all types of patients, from premature infants to geriatric patients, and with all kinds of diagnoses. This covers anything that limits patients' ability to care for themselves—arthritis, injuries, burns, neurological dysfunction. Such patients may be stroke victims or have multiple sclerosis, muscular dystrophy, cerebral palsy, brain tumors, or psychiatric problems. Occupational therapists work in the following settings:

- Acute-care hospitals
- Rehab hospitals
- Psychiatric hospitals or wards
- Pediatric hospitals or wards
- Nursing homes
- School systems
- Private practice

## Training

Occupational therapists must earn a four-year degree, studying all the sciences, including zoology, biology, physiology, anatomy, and kinesiology. They also study psychology, abnormal psychology, and child development. Specialties can include pediatrics, psychiatry, hand therapy, and physical disabilities.

After four years of study, therapists complete a six- to nine-month internship, rotating in different kinds of facilities and specialties. After passing the internship, the next step is passing the national exam that is required to become a registered occupational therapist.

Some occupational therapists go on for master's degrees in occupational therapy or related fields, such as administration or physical therapy.

**Certified Occupational Therapy Assistants.** This position requires study at a community college toward a two-year associate's degree. Although associates don't evaluate patients or make treatment plans, they function much as physical therapy assistants do, carrying out the plans made by the occupational therapists.

Some universities have started weekend programs for occupational therapy assistants who want to work toward a four-year degree. While they are employed full-time, they study every other weekend, finishing the bachelor's degree in about two years.

**Occupational Therapy Aides.** Occupational therapy aides function similarly to their counterparts in physical therapy, helping the occupational therapists and assistants with various duties.

The personality qualities and skills needed to be a good occupational therapist or assistant are as follows:

- Be outgoing, with empathy and a good sense of humor.
- Be open and willing to talk with your patients.
- Be a good listener. Patients look to the therapist as someone they can talk to—doctors rarely have enough time for that kind of relationship.
- Have good people skills for dealing with coworkers and the family members of your patients.

**TABLE 4.4.** Therapy Professions: A Comparison of Jobs and Earnings

| JOB TITLE | NUMBER OF JOBS | ESTIMATED ANNUAL SALARY |
|---|---|---|
| Physical therapists | 80,000 | $54,810 |
| Physical therapy assistants | 44,000 | $33,870 |
| Physical therapy aides | 36,000 | $19,670 |
| Occupational therapists | 78,000 | $49,450 |
| Occupational therapy assistants | 17,000 | $34,340 |
| Occupational therapy aides | 8,500 | $20,710 |

Source: U.S. Department of Labor, Bureau of Labor Statistics, Occupational Outlook Handbook; numbers are for year 2000.

## Salaries

Salaries for occupational therapists are similar to those for physical therapists. In 2000, the median annual salary of occupational therapists was $49,450. Starting salaries for certified occupational therapy assistants average about $23,900. Occupational therapy aides earn a median $20,710 annually.

## Recreational Therapists

Recreational therapists employ activities to treat or maintain the physical, mental, and emotional well-being of patients. Activities range from sports and games to drama, arts and crafts, and music. Recreational therapists also often organize field trips, taking patients bowling, to sporting events, or on picnics.

Recreational therapists work in acute-care hospitals, psychiatric hospitals, nursing homes, and rehab centers. Community-based recreational therapists work in parks and recreation departments, special education programs, and programs for the elderly or the disabled.

In a clinical setting, recreational therapists work in conjunction with physicians, nurses, psychologists, social workers, and physical and occupational therapists.

Recreational therapists assess patients based on information in medical charts and from talking with other staff and family members as well as with the patients themselves. They then develop and carry out therapeutic activities consistent with the needs of the individual. For example, patients having difficulty with socialization skills may be included in games with other patients, or a right-handed person with a right-side paralysis after a stroke may be helped to use his or her left arm to swing a tennis racket or throw a softball.

## Training

A bachelor's degree in therapeutic recreation or in recreation with an option in therapeutic recreation is the usual requirement for hospital work and related clinical positions. Associate's degrees in recreational therapy; training in art, music therapy, or drama; or related work experience may be enough to qualify for activity director positions in nursing homes.

Courses students study include clinical practice and helping skills, program design, management, anatomy, physiology, abnormal psychology, medical and psychiatric terminology, characteristics of illness and disabilities, the concepts of mainstreaming and normalization, professional ethics, assessment and referral procedures, and the use of equipment.

In addition to the academics, recreational therapy students must participate in a 360-hour internship. After earning a bachelor's degree, new graduates take an examination administered by the National Council for Therapeutic Recreation Certification to become certified.

## Salaries

Recreational therapists generally start out in the high twenties or low thirties. Activity directors in nursing homes earn an average of $25,000 a year. A recent advertisement for a hospital-based therapist cited a $2,000 to $2,300 a month salary range. According to a survey conducted in 2000, median earnings for recreational therapists were $28,650. The top ten percent of therapists made more than $43,810.

Other career paths for therapists include mental health counseling and psychotherapy (Chapter 2) and horticultural therapy (Chapter 3).

# CHAPTER FIVE

# The World of Food

To a health nut, nothing is more important than eating good, healthful food. For health nuts hoping for a rewarding career related to their interests, there are many options in the world of food. Health nuts wanting to work with food can find careers growing and marketing food on organic farms; sharing information as extension agents; supplying customers with information as well as products in natural food stores and food co-ops; and preparing and serving healthful meals in restaurants. Other food-related careers include counseling people on diet and nutrition issues, discussed later in this chapter, and writing about food, which is highlighted in Chapter 6.

## Growing Food in Agricultural Careers

At the heart of our economic structure are American farmers, who operate one of the world's largest and most productive agricultural industries. This industry produces enough food to meet the needs of our country and to export vast quantities to countries around the world. Farms can be huge conglomerates or small, privately or cooperatively owned enterprises. Farmers can also be tenant farmers, renting the land they use.

Within the field of agriculture there are a number of different occupations. On the production side are the growers, owners, managers, and field hands. Once the food has been harvested, experienced handlers store it, then pack and ship it. Distributors handle sales and marketing, and retailers, such as restaurants and supermarkets, sell to the public.

The specific tasks for growers are determined by the type of farm. On traditional crop farms, operators are responsible for planning, tilling, planting, fertilizing, cultivating, spraying, and harvesting. Organic farmers, who do not use chemicals in their operations, must also seek out alternative ways to fight pests and disease and increase production.

On large farms, owners or managers spend time meeting with supervisors and traveling between the fields and their offices.

## Training for Farmers

Modern farming requires complex scientific, business, and financial decisions. Today's farmer must acquire a strong educational background. No longer is it enough to grow up on a farm or participate as a youth in 4-H activities, though these are important contributors to an overall education.

For those who have no previous farming experience, a bachelor's degree in agriculture is essential. To qualify as a manager, several years' experience in different phases of farm operation are also necessary. Students should choose a college appropriate to their specific interests and locations. All states have land-grant colleges with agriculture departments. For crop growers, courses would cover agricultural economics, crop and fruit science, and soil science.

Farm operators and managers need to keep informed about continuing advances in farming methods. They should be willing to try new techniques and adapt to constantly changing technologies that can help produce or enhance their crops. They should also be familiar with the different farm machinery and its safe use, chemicals and their applications, and organic alternatives to pesticides and chemical fertilizers.

Accounting and bookkeeping are also important skills. And these days, more and more farms are depending upon computers to keep track of accounts and crop production and distribution, so farm managers often need to have business skills, good communication skills, and marketing and sales experience.

## Salaries

Income for farmers can vary from year to year. Food prices fluctuate from week to week and are affected by the weather and other factors that influence the demand for certain products. The size and type of the farm also affects income. Generally, large farms produce more income than smaller operations. The exceptions to that are the specialty farms that produce small amounts of high-value horticultural and fruit products.

According to the U.S. Department of Agriculture, average income after expenses for vegetable and fruit farms was $100,000 in 1993. Individual income can vary widely. In general, surveys of all types of farms—traditional and organic—show that farm managers earned a median $542 per week in 2000. These are very general numbers. The amount of money a farm earns depends greatly on the kind of products growing, the size of the operation, and innumerable other factors.

Seasonal workers usually earn minimum wage, or about $5 an hour. The growers within a cooperative earn different amounts depending upon the size of their property or what kind of year they had. The earnings could range from just $1,000 to about $35,000 or $40,000 in gross sales.

Many people don't realize how much it costs to grow food. In addition to worker's wages, the farmer also has to pay off whatever loans were taken out for necessary farm equipment as well as the mortgage on the farm itself, which leaves little left over for the farmer's salary.

Because the work for some farmers and managers is seasonal, and the income fluctuates so, many growers take second jobs during the off months. If a couple owns and runs a farm, it's not unusual that one of them works an additional job to help support the family.

## Job Outlook

Employment overall of traditional farmers and ranchers is expected to decline through the year 2010. With an expanding world population there is an increasing demand for food, but because of the productivity of the American agricultural sector, fewer farms are needed to meet that demand. The overwhelming majority of job openings will come about because of the need to replace farmers who retire or leave the occupation for economic or other reasons.

The trend toward fewer but larger farms is expected to continue to reduce the number of jobs. Small and medium-size farms, many of which do not generate enough income to support their owners, are expected to decrease in number.

However, the increase in the size of farms, generally through mergers, and the higher level of technology being employed in farm work are expected to spur a need for highly trained and experienced farm managers. And there's an intriguing niche opportunity for operators of organic farms. More agricultural managers, farmworkers, and sorters will be needed, but these vocations will see their numbers rise at a slower rate than other industries; however, agricultural services, including animal care and veterinary professions, will grow 39 percent by 2010, much faster than average, and so will biotechnology, a high-tech research field closely related to agriculture and the science of growing things.

........................................

## Organic Farming

Organic farming is an exciting, and burgeoning, facet of the American farming landscape. While it has a long history within the farming community, this movement gained further legitimization in October 2002, when the Federal Organic Certification Standards went into effect. These standards establish the criteria that must be met in order for food to be labeled "organic." As a testament to the growing demand from the public for more organic food, 2001 marked the first year in which supermarkets sold more organic food than organic specialty stores.

The size of the organic food industry in America is growing accordingly to keep up with demand. The amount of organic cropland doubled between 1992 and 1997, the total number of organic farms grew by 40 percent from 1992 to 2001, and $7.8 billion was spent on organic food by consumers in 2000, according to U.S. Department of Agriculture research.

## An Organic Cooperative Enterprise

Some good examples of successful organic food farms are the members of the Finger Lakes Organic Growers, a cooperative enterprise with approximately thirty active members. Most of the farms, which are spread across New York State, are fifteen acres or smaller. The growers purchased shares in the cooperative; in exchange, the cooperative markets their produce for them. Their aim is to grow all their crops organically without the use of any chemical pesticides or fertilizers. They are committed to sustainable agriculture, meaning they farm in such a way that the environment benefits from it—the soil gets richer, and the general ecology is preserved.

Carol Stull is one of the founding members of the Finger Lakes Organic Growers Cooperative, which began operation in 1986. A group of about six growers had been meeting and talking about how handling their own selling, in addition to the farming, was a hassle. Several of their regular customers would buy one thing from one farmer and if that farmer ran out, they'd go to someone else. The farmers realized that both they and their customers would benefit if their resources could be brought together.

"We had been talking about it for a year and then one of the growers said, 'Let's do it and here's my $5 to start,'" explains Carol. The group applied for a grant from New York State Agriculture and Markets and received $15,000 in start-up money for the cooperative. This initial investment was used to set up a computer program and rent a truck for deliveries. They had a market manager who worked out of her living room. During the first year, the cooperative didn't have a warehouse but used a farm that belonged to one of the growers and brought things there or to a couple of pickup points. The grant money was also used to pay an artist to develop a logo, to get office supplies, and to cover employees' salaries.

Each member of the cooperative has his or her own farm. After getting advice from a Vista volunteer who worked with another cooperative, they learned that they should set up a personnel committee so each grower wasn't telling the manager something different to do. Each gave up all wholesale markets to the co-op. The manager now takes care of all the selling, which used to take at least one-quarter of each farmer's time—and that wasn't enough time to do an effective job.

The Finger Lakes Organic Growers cooperative now employs a full-time marketing manager, an assistant manager, and a warehouse manager who is responsible for quality control and putting the orders together to go out on the trucks. The work is seasonal, and the managers are on shorter schedules in the winter.

The marketing manager's main function is to do the marketing and advertising for the cooperative and try to expand the business. The board of directors meets once a month to do long-term strategic planning with the recommendations of the various managers. If they decide they want to increase new customers by 20 percent, for example, then it's the marketing manager's job to decide how to do that.

The cooperative supplies produce to restaurants, supermarkets, retail food co-ops, and natural food stores, and to other wholesalers when there is a surplus of something. For example, zucchini tends to grow all at once, so sometimes they have so much that they can lower the price and make it appealing to other wholesalers who might not have enough supply. The marketing manager shares information with the customers who call about what's moving well or not moving at different food co-ops. There are always trends; for example, asparagus might gain steadily in popularity, while chard becomes less and less popular. The marketing manager also takes the orders and keeps track of inventory to make sure the cooperative is not running out of things.

The warehouse manager collects the invoices, packs the orders, collects the boxes from the cooler, and stacks them together on a truck pallet, ready to be delivered. Then the trucker loads up and drives off.

## Carol's Individual Farm

Carol and her husband bought their land in Ithaca, New York, in 1985. "Our business was only a year old when we started the cooperative. Before that we used to market our produce direct at farmer's markets. We were small, just learning to go from packets to pounds. You buy a packet of seeds for a small home garden, but when you're growing commercially you buy seeds by the pound. We have sixty-five acres and farm about ten acres of it. We grow all of the standard vegetables, except corn.

"One of the benefits to being a small, independent farmer is the freedom that it grants you. Some farmers gain entrance into the wholesale restaurant market by growing edible flowers or unusual cherry tomatoes that others don't grow.

The number of employees on a small farm such as Carol's fluctuates. In the summer students help with the planting and picking. A job that would be impossible for the farm's owners to complete becomes quite manageable with a small team of seasonal workers.

Advance planning is definitely required on a small organic farm. You have to know where you're going to plant each crop, and what was planted there in the past. Some farms work on a three-year rotation, which means they don't plant crops from the same family in the same place in the field for three years.

Some farms also have greenhouses, enabling them to extend their growing seasons and provide out-of-season produce to customers. In addition to selling her produce through a cooperative, Carol sells at the local farmer's market on Saturdays and has a roadside stand on her property. "When you have more cherry tomatoes than you absolutely know what to do with, you look at every market available."

## The Cooperative Extension Service

While now only about 3 or 4 percent of Americans live in agricultural areas and rural settings, in the early 1900s the United States was largely an agrarian society. At that time approximately 40 percent of the population was spread out in rural areas, and the rest resided in urban centers. The farmers felt they needed more information about agriculture in order to do a better job feeding the nation.

A number of issues were brought before Congress at the time to help the nation's agricultural interests. First, a bill was passed forming land-grant colleges so that every state would have a college, technical in nature, with its main focus to conduct research in agriculture. Second, Congress recognized the need for physical locations in which to conduct related research. Because of the type of research needed, it couldn't be done in a laboratory; it had to be done out in the field. This brought about the establishment of research stations associated with each land-grant college. They were located at or near the universities—wherever crops were grown. Some states established several research stations. Third, it was realized that with all this new research and knowledge being gained, there needed to be a way to disseminate the information. This is how the Cooperative Extension Service began.

The name *cooperative* was chosen because the program is funded with state, county, and federal monies. Every county has at least one, if not more, programs. An advisory board for each county points out areas that need to be addressed and services that need to be offered.

The function of the Cooperative Extension Service has since expanded beyond agricultural issues and now also covers home economics, the 4-H youth program, and a program that helps commercial fisheries. The Cooperative Extension Service works with the community to bring the research that's done at the universities to the public where it's needed. To do this, the Cooperative Extension Service employs professional agricultural specialists, horticulturists, and educators as Cooperative Extension agents.

## Becoming a Cooperative Extension Agent

An extension agent is an employee of the land-grant college and the county. The position requires a master's degree in whatever field is appropriate—vegetable science, agriculture, entomology, sociology, pathology, or any related subjects.

There is a growing need for policy-making agents, or people who work with the community on environmental issues. What the agents do is determined by the needs of the county. Where wheat is grown, the agent needs to be a wheat specialist. Where there are cows, a veterinary medicine background is needed. The number of agents varies with the county, and agents may handle topics as diverse as home economics, youth activities, fishing programs, and urban and agricultural horticulture.

Every office also has a director to whom the extension agents report. To become a director, a master's degree is required as well as several years' experience working as an extension agent.

Willingness to work hard is a requirement, as you're often on call at all hours. If there's a hurricane or heavy rain or some disaster, extension agents are expected to help and answer questions about what people should do in those situations. Because of this and the dependency people have on these workers to help them out in tough situations, the work can be stressful.

## Salaries

Salaries follow state and county scales and vary from region to region. An affiliated agent with a bachelor's degree would expect to earn in the high teens. A new agent just out of graduate school could expect to earn $20,000 to $25,000 a year. After a few years of experience, salaries increase with cost-of-living and merit raises. In 2001, the national average for all extension agents was $45,350, according to USDA figures.

Although the Cooperative Extension Service has a national office in Washington, D.C., there is no national job bank. Positions are usually posted at the land-grant colleges, and the individual county offices are then notified.

Contacting the state university is the best place to start. You can find your local Extension Office in the telephone book under county or state government offices. For those seeking a career with the Extension Service, it's a good idea to be prepared to relocate. You can decide upon an area of the country in which you would like to work, making sure you are familiar with the different horticultural requirements of that area. Then call the various land-grant colleges for job openings.

## A Cooperative Extension Service Agent

Loretta Hodyss has been an extension agent in Palm Beach County, Florida, since 1979. In a county like Palm Beach with a population of 900,000, perhaps only 10,000 are associated with agriculture and the rest are urban. The largest component of an agent's work in this setting is urban horticulture. Loretta might answer people's questions about their lawns or how to grow a certain plant on the window sill or how to grow vegetables, trees, or shrubs. While the service is free to the public, there may be a charge for some publications and classes to cover expenses.

Loretta works mainly with the county's commercial nursery industry. "I spend my time answering questions, helping them with their crop problems—mostly insect- and disease-related issues. In Palm Beach County it's a $200 million industry. We have six hundred nurseries, which keeps me pretty busy."

Some of Loretta's work is done over the telephone. The service is open for questions from the public from nine to five, Monday through Friday. Loretta frequently makes visits to nurseries to provide information and answer questions. The service also offers various educational programs, different sorts of classes, newsletters, and published material for distribution.

Loretta likes having a challenging job with something different to do every day. "There's always something new and interesting to learn, and you're constantly encouraged to go back to school and learn. There is a wealth of information out there—and a wealth of people who are appreciative of your help.

"My role is that of educator more than anything else. Many of us do research, also. We've struggled with the title—we'd rather be called extension educators than extension agents, and in some states they have changed it."

## Natural Food Stores

Natural food stores are specialty shops that cater to health nuts, selling a wide range of healthful foods and related items, such as vitamins and food supplements. Typically, these markets stock health-oriented products and offer organic produce, organic foods, and nonorganic frozen foods and groceries. They avoid foods made with preservatives, refined sugars, or additives, and generally do not sell any food that has been irradiated to prolong its shelf life.

Customers are people with special diet or health needs, and those who just live a natural, healthy lifestyle, including vegans and vegetarians. Stores may have a café or a vegan deli or may cater to sports enthusiasts and body builders by stocking several lines of sports drinks and powders and different types of vitamins and formulas. In addition, stores may carry environmentally safe cleaning products that are biodegradable with no harsh chemicals.

Employees in natural food stores must be knowledgeable about the different foods and products and be able to answer a wide range of customer questions. The duties of a manager vary from store to store. The job often entails doing a little of everything: ordering, taking out garbage, cleaning bathrooms, ringing up sales, working on store operating policies, supervising employees, and talking to brokers, sales reps, and distributors.

Dealing with customers involves interacting with those who are very knowledgeable—sometimes even more knowledgeable than the staff—and customers who are visiting a health food store for the first time and don't know what they should buy. A store manager needs to be customer service–oriented and promote that attitude in the staff.

Being a store manager, even in a health food store, can lend itself to stress. You have employees under you, an owner above you, customers, all kinds of salespeople, and you're being pulled in a lot of different directions, so you need to be patient as well as interested in health to be good at this job.

## Getting the Job and Salary Statistics

Many health food stores are very open to training new employees, but they do look for certain qualities in job candidates, including a good attitude, a strong interest, and willingness to learn.

In addition to scanning help-wanted ads, job seekers should stop by the stores where they would like to work.

Entry-level salaries usually are quite low, from $5 to $6 an hour, depending on your knowledge and skills and the area of the country in which you work. Nationally, grocery store salespeople took home $7.92 an hour as a median wage in 2000. Butchers and bakers earned more, and managers could earn as much as $21 an hour. As you climb up the ladder, the pay scale doesn't necessarily climb with you. You're in the health food business to be in the health food business, and not necessarily for the money.

# Diet and Nutrition

Health nuts interested in this specialization find employment as dietitians or nutritionists in hospitals, schools, day-care centers, summer camps, hotels, natural food stores, and weight-loss clinics. They can also set themselves up in private practice.

Historically, though, dietitians have been thought of as the professionals who work in hospitals. Nutritionists are thought of more as working in the community on an outpatient basis, counseling for nutritional problems or weight loss. They also work in health food stores, helping customers with nutritional concerns. Basically, the two terms carry the same weight, as long as both professionals have gone through similar training programs and are licensed by the state.

## The Role of Registered Dietitians and Nutritionists

There are several different kinds of dietitians with a wide variety of duties.

**Clinical Dietitians.** Clinical dietitians generally work in a hospital setting in a patient-oriented role. Each dietitian is usually assigned one or two floors, about fifty patients per dietitian.

Clinical dietitians visit patients, review their medical records, and evaluate their nutritional status to determine what would be the best diet for them to be on given their specific medical problems. They look at the chart to see what the patients were admitted for and what kind of lab results they had. They interview the patients, asking about their diet history, what they usually eat, whether they've been following any special diets or have lost weight recently, if they have any trouble swallowing or chewing, and so forth. That information is then recorded in the medical record before it gets processed in the diet office, where the menus originate. Afterward, it is passed to the kitchen so patients can be fed appropriate meals three times a day. Dietitians work with regular diets or design diets with restrictions for patients with ailments such as diabetes, renal or cardiac problems, or cancer.

**Specialized Dietitians.** These professionals work with special-needs patients, such as those in kidney dialysis centers, where diet plays a major role in the treatment of the patient. They deal with tube feedings or parenteral nutrition, when a patient is fed a concentrated formula of carbohydrates and protein through a large vein.

**Administrative Dietitians**. These individuals oversee the entire food service operation, from purchasing, storing, and preparing food to all other functions of the kitchen.

**Community Dietitians**. Community dietitians or nutritionists work with patients on an outpatient basis in health food stores, clinics, or private practice. They counsel patients to help them lose weight, bring down their cholesterol levels, deal with food allergies, or handle a variety of other concerns.

**Dietetic Technicians**. Registered dietitians, especially in large and busy hospitals, depend on the help of registered dietetic technicians, or diet techs, as they are called. Most diet techs are clinically oriented and do basic screenings of patients, review medical records, and document their findings on the patient charts. They generally handle the less complicated cases, leaving specialized patient needs to registered dietitians. Diet techs can also work in nursing homes, overseeing the food service operation or working in the kitchen.

**Diet Aides and Nutrition Assistants**. Diet aides function in a clerical role. They write the patient's name and room number on the menus, pass menus out to the patients on the floors, and wait while the different preferences are checked. They then review the menus, making sure they've been marked properly.

## Training for Dietitians

A dietitian must have a four-year degree in foods and nutrition from an accredited university. The course work covers a lot of science—biology, chemistry, physiology—as well as nutrition, math, foods, and food science. A six- to nine-month supervised internship is also required. Some programs allow the internship to run concurrently with the senior year; in other programs the internship can be started only after graduation. After the internship, students are eligible to take a registration exam administered by the American Dietetic Association, the national professional organization. Some dietitians go on to earn master's degrees, especially if they are interested in administrative positions or want to maintain their competitiveness for jobs.

Diet techs usually earn two-year degrees in foods and nutrition from community colleges. They are then eligible to take an exam administered by the American Dietetic Association to become registered dietetic technicians. Many then find jobs and continue to study on the weekends to earn their four-year degrees.

Diet aides and nutrition assistants usually have no formal training in foods and nutrition. They must have a high school diploma and have good written and verbal skills. The work is mainly clerical, and most are trained on the job. Becoming a diet aide is a good way to get a taste for the profession, so to speak. After spending some time in a hospital food department, you can then decide if you want to go on for further training.

## The Hours You'll Work

Your shifts will vary depending upon the setting, but for the most part dietitians avoid weekend work and the late night and overnight shifts that many nurses must deal with. But some dietitians are on call over the weekend and must come in for emergencies. Diet techs and assistants aren't as lucky, and generally they pull regular weekend duty. For diet aides, the earliest shift starts about 5:30 A.M. in order to help serve breakfast. They finish about 2:30 in the afternoon. The latest shift ends at about 7:30 in the evening after the dinner meal is over.

## Salaries

As with most professions, salaries vary depending upon the region of the country and the size of the institution's hiring budget.

Registered dietitians usually are paid an annual salary. The median income for dietitians is $38,450, based on year 2000 figures. For entry-level candidates, that could begin in the mid-twenties and increase with more experience. In hospitals, the job setting with the most opportunity for dietitians, the median income of $39,450 is slightly better than that in other job settings. Administrators, depending upon their responsibilities, could earn from $30,000 to $80,000 a year, and diet techs generally start in the low twenties. Diet aides are usually paid hourly, from $5.50 to $7.00.

The benefits of working in a hospital usually make up for the low pay. This includes good health-care plans, pensions, vacation days, sick leave, holidays, and personal days.

## A Day in the Life of a Dietitian

Emily Friedland is the assistant director of food and nutrition at Boca Raton Community Hospital in Boca Raton, Florida. She has a B.S. in nutrition and foods from Cornell University and an M.A. in food service management from New York University.

Emily is responsible for the entire department, which has about one hundred employees. The department is made up of different sections—patient feeding, cafeteria feeding, visitor coffee shop, and clinical nutrition. In the clinical nutrition area Emily directly supervises a total of twenty-five dietitians, diet techs, and nutrition aides.

"I review their work, maintain and update a diet manual, which is all the different diets our patients might be on, and write and implement policies and procedures. My job is varied; it's different each day. We have an in-service training program, so every month there are one or two classes we present, and we are continually measuring the quality of our performance.

"I enjoy being in a management position. You never know what you're going to face when you walk in the door in the morning. There are always different crises that come up—a piece of equipment is broken, or someone didn't show up to work. In the food service industry you are committed to getting those three meals out every day. You have to put out a product no matter what.

"There's a lot of variety. There are always new cases, different needs—it doesn't get boring. The registered dietitian is getting more involved in the complicated cases now. Our dietitians are being more and more specialty trained, and the physicians see that this person really knows what he or she is talking about.

"Sometimes people are reluctant to spend money to consult a dietitian. But the upside is it's a great job if you enjoy working in a health-care setting, working with people, but don't want to do hands-on care. And if you enjoy the relationship between food and health, you're able to put that into practice."

## Health Inspectors

The world of food includes growers, preparers, servers, sales-people, and dietary and nutritional consultants. But there are a few additional food-related careers that could also appeal to health nuts.

Health inspectors work with engineers, chemists, microbiologists, health workers, and lawyers to ensure compliance with public health and safety regulations governing food, drugs, cosmetics, and other consumer products. There are several types of inspector positions that would interest health nuts.

- **Food inspectors** inspect meat, poultry, and their by-products to ensure they are safe for public use. They observe slaughtering, processing, and packaging operations and check for product labeling and proper sanitation.
- **Consumer safety inspectors** specialize in food, feeds, pesticides, weights and measures, cosmetics, drugs, and medical equipment. Some are proficient in more than one specialization. Working individually or in teams, they periodically check firms that produce, handle, store, and

market the products they regulate. They look for inaccurate labeling or chemical or bacteriological contamination that could result in a product becoming harmful to health.

- **Agricultural quarantine inspectors** protect American agriculture from the spread of foreign plant and animal pests and diseases. They inspect ships, airplanes, trains, and motor vehicles entering the United States, looking for restricted or prohibited plants, animals, insects, agricultural commodities, and animal by-products.
- **Agricultural commodity graders** apply quality standards to ensure that retailers and consumers know the quality of the products they purchase. They inspect eggs, meat, poultry, fruit and vegetables, grain, tobacco, cotton, and dairy products. After determining quality and grade, they issue official grading certificates.
- **Environmental health inspectors** ensure that food, water, and air meet government standards. They may specialize in dairy products, food sanitation, waste control, air or water pollution, institutional sanitation, or occupational health. They check the safety and cleanliness of food produced in dairies and processing plants or served in restaurants, hospitals, and other institutions.

## Training

Educational requirements vary with the job, generally requiring college or technical training, at a minimum, through advanced degrees in environmental engineering for the most sophisticated jobs. In addition, specialized certification is often required. This can be obtained through agencies such as the Board of Certified Safety Professionals (BCSP) and the American Board of Industrial Hygiene (ABIH). These groups provide training toward the Certified Safety Professional (CSP) credential or the Certified Industrial Hygienist (CIH) credential. The Council on Certification of Health, Environmental, and Safety Technologists, a joint venture of the two groups, oversees the Occupational Health and Safety

Technologist (OHST) certification. Each specialized profession has its own credentialing body. To read more about careers related to the environment, see Chapter 7.

## Getting That Job

Information on jobs with the federal government is available from state employment offices, area offices of the U.S. Office of Personnel Management, and Federal Job Information Centers in large cities throughout the country. For information on specific inspector jobs, you may also contact the federal department or agency that employs them. Information about state and local government jobs is usually available from state civil service commissions, usually located in each state capital, or from local government offices. Information about jobs in the private sector is available from the state employment service, listed in your telephone directory.

## Salaries

Agricultural inspectors were earning a median income of $13.75 an hour in 2001. Current (2003) data from the U.S. Office of Personnel Management shows average annual salaries for a few selected inspector positions as follows:

| | |
|---|---|
| Environmental protection specialists | $69,307 |
| Public health quarantine inspectors | $63,675 |
| Agricultural commodity graders | $42,333 |
| Food inspectors | $33,973 |

A survey of the salaries of all occupational health and safety specialists, technicians, and inspectors showed a $42,750 median annual income in 2000.

## Job Outlook

Employment for inspectors—occupational health and safety specialists and technicians—is expected to increase as fast as the average for all occupations through the year 2010, reflecting growing public demand for a safe environment and quality products. In 2002, there were thirty-five thousand jobs nationwide in these categories. Many were with federal and state governments.

The level of need for inspectors is affected by legislation and by enforcement activities. However, manufacturing-sector inspections are now often automated, so in that sector, opportunities will decline. Construction-sector jobs will grow at an average rate, along with the economy. Occupational health and safety technicians and inspectors will continue to be needed in response to the level of public demand for environmental and workplace quality of life.

# CHAPTER SIX

# The Health Beat

Health nuts who combine their knowledge and love of good health, food, fitness, and a clean environment with a talent for writing can bring in extra income or land themselves a full-time career writing or reporting about health issues. With a thorough grasp of the subject, an understanding of the needs of book publishers and magazine and newspaper editors—and a lot of drive and persistence—dedicated health nuts can teach others what they know through the written word.

## Writing How-To and Self-Help Books

Investigate any bookstore or your local library and you'll find hundreds of volumes covering every aspect of the world of health, fitness, and medicine, from cooking and eating healthfully to spiritual and physical healing and a range of topics in between.

These how-to books can be very successful, and publishers are always on the lookout for new projects that take a fresh approach. Here are just a few successful topics:

- Eating well
- Exercising
- Holistic medicine
- Living well
- Psychology and relationships
- Recovery
- Reference

## Getting Started

When deciding what to write about, it's a good idea to find a topic that hasn't been overdone. An overlooked subject, the results of new research, or a new slant or twist on an old subject can work; the trick is to find a hole in the marketplace, a gap that only your book can fill.

If you've come across a gap and thought of the perfect idea for a book to fill it, don't worry if you think your experience or knowledge is too limited. Very few writers can put together a book without doing research or interviewing experts in the field. Professional associations can direct you to members who would be willing to help (see Appendix A for a list of associations).

## Developing a Proposal

After you've developed your idea and have checked to make sure it brings something new to the market, you need to prepare a book proposal. Your proposal should explain your topic, why your book has something different to offer, who will buy your book, and what format your book will take. You'll need a table of contents, a sample chapter or two, and an outline of the remaining chapters. An excellent resource to guide you is Michael Larsen's book, *How to Write a Book Proposal* (Writer's Digest Books.) In addition to explaining the proper format and content for a book proposal, it also helps you decide whether your idea is a viable one.

## What to Do with Your Book Proposal

While you study the variety of titles already out there, take note of the particular publishing houses that put them in print. You should send your book proposal to publishers who handle your topic. You can write to the various publishers for their catalogs, which will give you an idea of their full range and will show you where your title might fit in their lists. You can also study the *Writer's Market* (Writers Digest Books), an annual guide that lists publishers and their needs and submission requirements.

Some writers prefer to concentrate on their writing (and related health interests) and work with agents who handle the selling side. Finding an agent can take almost as much time as finding a publisher, but in the end, it is well worth the effort. A good agent knows what projects will fit with which publishers—and which will not. You can find an agent through the *Literary Marketplace* (R.R. Bowker), available at your library, or through Writer's Digest's *Guide to Literary Agents*. You can also write to the Association of Authors' Representatives (see Appendix A) for a list of its member agents. AAR members agree to adhere to a specific code of ethics; the AAR's list, however, does not specify areas of interest.

## What Happens Next?

Once your proposal has been submitted to a publisher, the waiting begins. If your project grabs the right editor's interest, if you've presented your subject well and have made a convincing argument for the viability of your project, and if you're lucky, you might be asked to submit the completed manuscript for consideration. The best-case scenario would be an acceptance based upon your proposal. Successful writers know that there are two keys to joining the ranks of published authors:

1. An interesting and well-executed manuscript/proposal
2. Persistence

If your idea is a good one, the quality of your work is exceptional, and you don't give up easily, approaching a publisher can eventually pay off. You can ask for an advance, once the idea is accepted, so you can pay the bills while you work on the project.

## Profile of an Author

David Hirsch has been with the Moosewood Restaurant, a collectively run vegetarian eating establishment in Ithaca, New York, for nearly twenty years and is the author of *The Moosewood*

*Restaurant Kitchen Garden,* a practical guide to creative gardening for the adventurous cook. While sharing his personal experiences with the reader, David gives instructions for growing and harvesting, creating garden design plans, and using more than thirty vegetables and thirty-five herbs, including edible flowers and gourmet vegetables. The book has been well received, with more than fifty thousand copies in print.

David talks about his book and how he got started: "For me there was always a very strong connection between the process of growing and cooking, and these are two areas that strongly interest me. I love to garden and I love to cook. It seemed as if it would be a very enjoyable project, to take two things I cared about and knew a fair amount about and write about them.

"We already had literary agents because of the other Moosewood books, and they suggested I write a proposal. I put it together, and they submitted it to Simon & Schuster. It's always nice to make money at something you love, but as with any job, there are always some stresses or concerns. For me, there was certainly the concern of writing a whole book by myself. But I did get a lot of support. Other Moosewood people helped out and tested my recipes. Writing requires a real commitment of time and space to get it done. You have deadlines hanging over your head all the way through. The publishers want half the manuscript by a certain date, the remaining half by another date. Then you send it in and they send it back to you with suggestions for changes as well as another deadline they want to receive everything by. So you have to set up that discipline in your life.

"A lot of people who aren't full-time writers are doing something else with their time. You have to work around that, to fit everything in."

## Writing for Magazines and Newspapers

For those of you who feel tackling a book-length project seems too overwhelming, at least at first, you can always start with magazine and newspaper articles. Pick an area that interests you, an area you want to learn more about, because with most writing projects you have to do some research. You need to know something about the subject; you need to have something to say.

There are hundreds of magazines that, if not entirely devoted to health and fitness, include some kind of health or lifestyle articles for their readership. Take a look at any good-size newsstand; make note of health and fitness magazines, then flip through other general-interest publications to see which ones also include articles on the same subjects.

The *Writer's Market*, in addition to listing book publishers and their requirements, also contains a hefty selection of both trade and consumer publications.

Most major and many local newspapers have health or lifestyle sections or columns. Abalone Press has compiled a computerized directory of the nation's largest dailies, complete with the names of nearly two thousand key editors. It is formatted to work with whatever word processing or database program you use, and it can save you hours of unnecessary typing while sending out multiple submissions. For more information, contact:

Abalone Press
14 Hickory Avenue
Takoma Park, MD 20912

## How to Get Started Freelancing

You don't have to work full-time for a publication to write health-related articles; most magazines use a good number of freelance submissions each month. Most freelancers work as independent contractors, setting up a home office, sending out article ideas or completed manuscripts, negotiating payment, and setting their own hours. Of course, there are deadlines to meet as well as high standards for the work to be publishable.

Editors want to see well-written, informative articles that will be of interest to their readers. A good article should have a strong lead and a body filled with examples, anecdotes, and quotes from experts.

## Approaching Editors

There are different ways to approach a publication. The method you choose should follow the preferences the editors have expressed in the various market books or in their own guidelines for writers. To get a copy of a magazine's guidelines, send your request with a self-addressed, stamped envelope (SASE).

It is also a good idea to have read the magazine for which you would like to write so you are familiar with its format and style. If you can't find the magazine at a newsstand, you can write to the publisher for a sample copy.

The first rule when approaching a magazine is to make sure your letter is addressed to a specific editor by name. You can find this information in the magazine's masthead or listed in the *Writer's Market.*

A few editors prefer to see completed manuscript submissions, but most editors don't want to see an entire article right away; they would rather you send them a query letter. A query letter is a mini-proposal, stating the topic about which you would like to write, how you would approach it, and what qualifies you to write it. The query letter gives the editor an idea of your writing style and helps him or her decide quickly whether the subject matter is right for the publication. You might be proposing an article the magazine has already covered or has plans to cover with a different writer. Query letters save everyone time.

If an editor likes your query, you'll probably receive a letter asking to see the completed manuscript. New freelancers just breaking in often have to write the article "on spec" with no guarantee of publication. Once you have some publishing credits under your belt, a query letter can lead to a paid assignment.

Once your piece has been accepted, be prepared to wait several months before it sees print, although newspapers usually have a faster turnaround time than magazines. Health websites need content, too, and they work on a faster schedule and sometimes pay faster, if your writing is right for them. It's another alternative that may contribute to positive cash flow.

## Some Sample Markets

In addition to a wide variety of national magazines that cover everything from tofu to tennis elbow, most states have regional magazines that include health or lifestyle features. The following are two sample publications that accept articles health nuts would enjoy writing:

- *Men's Health* publishes articles with a male slant, taking a broad view of health to cover both the physical and emotional. It includes profiles, exposés, and articles about relationships, eating right, and clinics that deal with specific health problems. Payment is twenty-five to sixty cents a word. Send submissions to Rodale Press, 33 East Minor Street, Emmaus, PA 18098; www.menshealth.com.
- *Vegetarian Times* uses articles with a vegetarian slant. It covers cooking, diet, lifestyle, health, consumer choices, natural foods, and environmental concerns. Payment is twenty cents a word upon acceptance. Send query letters to Editorial Offices, 301 Concourse Boulevard, Suite 350, Glen Allen, VA 23059; www.vegetariantimes.com.

Find a copy of *Writer's Market* and page through it to see where your interests and talents as a freelancer can find a home. A new edition is published each year, with about eight thousand listings of publishers, magazines, newspapers, and other outlets for writing of all kinds, from poetry to TV scripts. You will want to get involved in local writers' groups as well to help you find the hidden job market, the local publications that are under the radar of big national directories such as *Writer's Market, Bacon's,* and *SRDS*. These groups include Author's Guild, P.E.N., and National Writers Union, to name only the largest national groups. See

Appendix A for a list of national and regional associations that may be helpful in your search. Specialty groups for health include the American Medical Writers Association and the Association of Health Care Journalists.

There are many other opportunities to meet with fellow writers, such as women's writers groups that focus on women's health issues, local chapters of Society of Professional Journalists, and public library–based writers workshops. Finally, there are many Internet "virtual" writers groups. No matter where you are, you need not feel isolated as a freelancer, if you don't want to be. Your work will improve as you talk to other writers—and see what the competition's up to!

## Landing Regular Assignments

Once you are established as a freelancer, you can often land regular assignments with the same editors. This can even turn into a permanent column in a magazine or newspaper. From there, you can syndicate yourself, selling the same column to noncompeting newspapers across the country.

Many people go into journalism knowing that they want to be medical writers. They can then plan their courses in school appropriately to get a good background. A combination of journalism and science and medicine courses is probably the best way to prepare for a career as a health and medical writer. There are even some people who have gone to medical school; one *New York Times* medical writer is an M.D., and many television stations have doctors who report on health-related issues.

## Earnings

**Freelance Pay.** Payment for one article varies from publication to publication but could range from $50 or so for small magazines to $200 or $300 and up to $1000 or more for national magazines. A survey by National Writers Union (*Freelance Writer's Guide*, Second Edition, 2000) showed consumer magazine pay rates in the range of $0.50 to $3.00 a word, or $500 to $3,000 for a thousand-word article. However, these are the top national magazines. National newspapers pay well also, in the range of $1.00 a word at the top end. Newspapers, regional or local, pay in the range of $0.15 to $0.40 a word. Trade (business-to-business) magazines pay in the range of $0.25 to $1.40 a word. There are many more trade magazines than there are top-flight consumer magazines. You have to find a niche, or work your way up the chain, to make a living as a freelancer.

Some magazines pay you as soon as they've accepted your manuscript; others wait until your article has been published. One trick to making enough money is to allow one article to bring in more than one fee. As long as the publications do not have a competing circulation, and you haven't sold all rights to the article, you can place your work in several publications in varying forms. For example, an article on healthful cooking could find homes in several regional magazines, as well as with local newspapers.

Reslanting an article to capture a broader audience can also help increase your income. An article for a children's magazine on how to eat well can be rewritten to address an adult audience. Reslanting increases the number of publications you can approach; resales increase your paycheck.

**Staff Salaries.** If you obtain a full-time job with a magazine or newspaper, the salaries vary, depending on the region you're in and the size of the organization. If you're just starting, you could find yourself in the low to mid-twenties range or less. Most small papers don't have dedicated health and medical writers; they rely on the wire services to provide stories.

With a few years' experience under your belt, you can move up the pay ladder to $30,000 or $40,000. With several years at a large newspaper, your salary could reach the $50,000 range.

Most of the time, before you could be hired at a large newspaper, you'd have to have experience at a smaller one. You can start off doing general assignments before you move on to your plum position somewhere else.

## A Health Writer

Nancy McVicar is a senior writer at the *Sun-Sentinel*, a newspaper in Fort Lauderdale, Florida, with a circulation of about one million. She works for the Lifestyle section, which has a health page every Thursday. Her stories also appear in other sections; recently a package of stories on the resurgence of infectious diseases began on the front cover.

Her articles focus on health, medicine, and fitness. Her work has been nominated for the Pulitzer Prize seven times, and several of her stories have won national awards.

Nancy talks about her job: "It's more than just medical writing. I look at questions such as why we need health-care reform and what it means to the average person. Another story I recently did was about how antibiotics are losing their effectiveness because we're overusing them. I wouldn't call it breaking news; it's more a trend story: here's something I think we need to be worried about, and why."

In researching stories there are a number of resources available. Newspapers often subscribe to various electronic databases and information services so that a writer can ask the resource center to do a search on what's been written in other publications about a particular subject.

"We can also get on the Internet and make queries about things. I was preparing to do an interview with Kristine Gebbie, the AIDS czar appointed by President Clinton, so I put out a question on the Internet asking people in the AIDS community what they would like to know from this woman. I got some really good suggestions for the interview. As it turned out, between the time I set it up and the time I actually did the interview, she resigned. It made an even better story about why she was quitting."

It can be useful to talk to doctors and others in the medical community and read a lot, particularly medical journals, or the journals and magazines pertinent to whatever field you are interested in. Medical writers may subscribe to *Journal of the American Medical Association*, the *New England Journal of Medicine*, and various other medical newsletters, from Johns Hopkins to the Mayo Clinic or the Lahey Clinic in Massachusetts. Consumer-oriented publications can also be good sources. *Consumer Reports* puts out a health letter, and the Center for Science in the Public Interest has a couple of publications, including one on nutrition.

"I also get a lot of phone calls from interested readers who say, 'I wonder if you know anything about such and such,' or 'I read there's a new treatment for high blood pressure and what can you tell me about it?' If I get enough calls on a particular subject I might decide there's an interest here that needs to be addressed and start researching it and do a story about it.

"Every once in a while I do a question-and-answer column, when I think it's called for. An outbreak of Hanta virus in the Southwest killed about half the people who got it. It's a deadly virus, and it turned up in South Dade. I did a Q&A to let readers know they didn't have to be too concerned, that it's not really contagious. You get it from breathing the dried-up urine of rodents that are infected.

"Finding ideas for stories is not my problem; finding time to do all the stories is the bigger problem. You can't do them in one afternoon. You have to use multiple sources. You have to call at least two or three experts, even though you might not end up quoting them all in the story. But you can never do a one-source medical story.

"I'll take a whole list of stories to my editor and we discuss them and decide which we should do first. We work with the photo people and our graphic staff so we can illustrate them.

"There's so much out there to write about," Nancy says, "that you can really pick and choose what you're interested in or what you think your readers will be interested in. It's not as if next week I'm going to be writing the same old story about some council meeting.

"And there is a wealth of experts to talk to who are willing to give you their time. But you have to know enough to be able to ask the right questions. You have to background yourself a bit before you get a doctor on the phone. You want to be able to ask intelligent questions and not waste his or her time."

. . . . . . . . . . . . . . . . . . .

## Lecturers

Writers in the field of health can supplement their incomes by taking to the lecture circuit. Authors of successful books are automatically considered experts on their subjects, and these experts are usually in demand to speak in a variety of settings, such as bookstores, colleges and universities, and community centers.

Lecture tours usually are arranged in conjunction with the release of a book and become part of the publisher's promotional efforts. In this case, payment to the lecturer would be in the form of royalties, a percentage of the price for each book sold.

Lecturers, either on their own or with the help of an agent or publicist, sometimes set up speaking engagements where an admission fee is charged. They are paid a set fee (which varies depending upon their popularity) or a percentage of the ticket receipts.

Successful lecturers generally have to be well-known figures with subjects that interest a wide audience.

. . . . . . . . . . . . . . . . . . . . . . . . . . .

## Photographers

Writers who can take their own photographs can often increase the amount of money they'll be paid for an article. A photographer with writing and/or marketing skills—and a focused project—can set out on his or her own to capture images of the American health scene. Photographers take still shots or videos of workout routines and exercise programs and illustrate books and articles in hundreds of other ways.

A highly specialized field in photography that would interest some creative health nuts is food photography. Food photographers are responsible for all the beautiful photographs you see in cookbooks and magazines or in television commercials.

## Training

Some photographers are self-taught, while others attend college or art school. Still others find a professional photographer with whom they can apprentice. Photographers need to become familiar with the technical as well as artistic aspects of photography. A part of any training program should include studying what other photographers produce.

Photographers with some market savvy also recognize the importance of acquiring good writing skills so they are able to write their own articles to go with their photographs, thus increasing their income.

## Salaries

Payment varies from assignment to assignment and from publication to publication. Sometimes a photographer is paid a set amount for each photograph that eventually sees print. That amount also varies depending on the size of the photograph— whether it fills a quarter, half, or full page. Photographs that make the cover of a magazine earn more.

Sometimes a photographer works for an hourly or daily rate. An editor might agree to pay for two full days of work at a set fee. If the assignment takes longer, the photographer doesn't earn any more money for that particular job. At the same time, if he or she spends less time than originally planned, the editor does not expect a refund.

In addition to their fees, photographers usually are paid for any additional expenses, such as travel and lodging or renting extra equipment or props.

# CHAPTER SEVEN

# Healing the Environment

**H**ealth nuts are concerned with more than just their own physical fitness and well-being. They realize that a healthy body and a healthy state of mind are possible only if the environment in which we all live is healthy, too.

Some careers you might be interested in that work toward that end include:

- Conservationist
- Educator
- Environmental engineer
- Environmentalist
- Forester
- Garden historian
- Land planner
- Landscape architect and designer
- Park ranger
- Range ecologist
- Researcher

## Working with the Land

The United States is filled with beautiful greenery, from the well-manicured lawns in suburban neighborhoods to public and private parks and forests. To design and maintain these areas, a growing number of residential, commercial, and government

**TABLE 7.1.** Environmental Job Options and Salaries

| JOB TITLE | NUMBER OF JOBS | MEDIAN SALARY | EDUCATION REQUIREMENTS |
|---|---|---|---|
| Environmental engineers | 52,000 | $57,780 | bachelor's/ graduate degree |
| Urban and regional planners | 30,000 | $46,500 | bachelor's/ graduate degree |
| Forestry and conservation workers | 21,000 | $8.97/hour | high school/ some college |

Source: U.S. Department of Labor, Bureau of Labor Statistics, Occupational Outlook Handbook. Numbers are national estimates for 2000 job market.

clients rely on the services of a wide range of horticulture, landscape, forest, and conservation specialists.

These specialists have the task of planning and caring for all kinds of land areas, paying attention to conservation and the impact on the environment as well as aesthetics.

## Land Planners

Land planners work in urban or rural settings devising plans that best utilize a community's land. They are knowledgeable about zoning and building codes and environmental regulations. Before preparing plans for long-range development, land planners conduct detailed studies that show current use. These reports include information concerning the location of streets, highways, water and sewer lines, public buildings, and recreational sites. This information allows them to propose ways of using undeveloped or underutilized land. Land planners then recommend layouts of buildings and other facilities, such as subway lines and stations. Land planners also have to show how the plans will be carried out and what they will cost.

Land planners divide their time between office work and on-site inspections. They also attend meetings and public hearings with citizens' groups.

## Employment for Land Planners

Two out of three land planners work for government planning agencies, from local city and county governments to state and federal agencies. Some of these federal agencies include the departments of defense, housing and urban development, and transportation.

Other planners do consulting or work full-time for firms that provide services to private developers or government agencies. Private-sector employers include management firms, architecture and surveying firms, educational institutions, and large land developers.

Salaries vary depending upon the hiring institution and the amount of education a land planner has pursued. Annual averages run $39,000 for bachelor's degree holders, $43,000 for those with master's degrees, and $57,000 for those with doctorates.

## What It Takes

Land planners can obtain graduate education in their chosen specialties, and in addition to their training in planning, landscape architecture, and civil engineering, they must also have excellent communication skills. Land planners work and interact with a variety of related professionals, including architects, city managers, environmental engineers, and geographers. They must also be able to negotiate with groups who may oppose the proposed development. An entire association devoted to the planning profession is the American Planning Association (see Appendix A).

.......................................

# Landscape Architects

Landscape architecture is the design of outside areas that are beautiful and functional as well as compatible with the natural environment. A landscape architect can work with small residential or commercial projects, or with complex projects on a much larger scale. These could include projects for cities or counties, industrial parks, historic sites, and a variety of other settings.

## Training

A bachelor's or master's degree is usually necessary for entry into the profession. Many bachelor's of landscape architecture (B.L.A.) programs take five years to complete; a master's degree can take another two or three years. The two-year master's program is designed for bachelor's-level landscape architects; the three-year program is for people with a bachelor's degree in a field other than landscape architecture. A master's degree helps refine your design abilities, focusing on more complex design problems. It also adds greatly to your employability and salary prospects.

Your college curriculum should include the following courses:

- History of landscape architecture
- Landscape design and construction
- Landscape ecology
- Structural design
- Drafting
- Urban and regional planning
- Design and color theory
- Soil science
- Geology
- Meteorology
- Topography
- Plant science and other introductory horticulture courses
- Civil engineering, including grading and drainage design
- Construction law and contracts
- General management

Almost all fifty states require landscape architects to be licensed. Licensing is based on passing the Landscape Architect Registration Examination (LARE), sponsored by the Council of Landscape Architecture Registration Boards. Admission to the exam usually requires a college degree and from one to four years or more of work experience. Some states, such as Florida and Arizona, require an additional exam focusing on state laws and the plant materials indigenous to that state. Landscape architects employed by the federal government are not required to be licensed.

Before licensing, a new hire typically is called a landscape architect intern. Interns work under the guidance of a licensed practitioner until they have passed the exam; however, they can, depending upon their employer's requirements, perform all the duties of a licensed landscape architect.

## Salaries

Statistics are limited, but in 1992 salaries for entry-level bachelor's degree landscape architects started at about $20,400 per year. Those with master's degrees were able to add another $10,000 to their annual salaries. By 2003, the median salary for a landscape architect was $43,540. New hires started at about $26,300, and veteran landscapers near the peak of their careers could make as much as $75,000.

# Historic Landscape Preservation and Garden History

Historic landscape preservation is a field of growing interest throughout the country among managers of historic buildings and cultural and natural landscapes. The Colonial Williamsburg Foundation in Williamsburg, Virginia, is a large employer of landscape architects, designers, and related groundskeeping professionals. Much of the research work involves looking at what was done historically in gardens: the kinds of plants that were grown, how gardens were laid out, and the types of fencing used. The research focuses on knowing how to recreate a historically accurate period-style garden.

A garden historian is someone who has a background in history and has researched the development of the historical landscape over time. Garden history is a specialty someone comes to within a general history curriculum. It's a young field that didn't start as a discipline in this country until 1975. Interested students combine history courses with horticulture courses.

The job market is fairly small, but it's growing. Right now most jobs are at living history museums, botanical gardens, or arboreta. These professionals work closely with the director in charge of maintenance, providing design expertise about what is needed in a particular garden. Once a decision has been made, the maintenance staff implements the work.

## Landscape Designers

A landscape designer works similarly to a landscape architect but usually on residential or small commercial projects. Landscape designers are not technically certified and cannot call themselves landscape architects.

For those who do not wish to invest the number of years it takes to become a landscape architect, a career in landscape design could be the answer. You can usually qualify to become a landscape designer after earning a two-year associate's degree in a landscape specialist program offered at a number of schools throughout the country.

Salaries are generally less for designers than for architects, but those who are self-employed are not as limited as those employed by a landscape architecture firm.

## Foresters and Conservationists

Forests and rangelands serve a variety of needs. They supply wood products, livestock forage, minerals, and water; serve as sites for recreational activities; and provide habitats for wildlife. Foresters and conservation scientists manage, develop, use, and help protect these and other natural resources.

Although many professional foresters and forest technicians spend a great deal of their time working outdoors during the first few years of their careers, there are many who do not. Duties outdoors include:

- Measuring and grading trees
- Evaluating insect outbreaks
- Conducting land surveys
- Fighting wildfires
- Laying out road systems
- Supervising construction of trails and planting of trees
- Supervising timber harvesting
- Conducting research studies

After a few years of on-the-ground experience, foresters can advance to administrative positions and then spend less time outside. These duties include planning, contracting, preparing reports, managing budgets, and consulting.

A professional forester has earned a four-year degree, while a forest technician normally holds an associate's degree in forest technology. Professional foresters concentrate on management skills, policy decisions, and the application of ecological concepts. Technicians generally work under a professional forester accomplishing day-to-day tasks.

Range managers—also called range conservationists, range ecologists, or range scientists—manage, improve, and protect rangelands to maximize their use without damaging the environment. Soil conservationists provide technical assistance to farmers and others concerned with the conservation of soil, water, and related natural resources. They develop programs to get the most use out of the land without damaging it.

## Training

In high school, future foresters should concentrate on basic mathematics, computer science, chemistry, botany, zoology, soil science, ecology, and related sciences. It is also important to develop good writing and public speaking skills.

A college degree is necessary, and those with a bachelor's degree will advance further and earn more than technicians with just an associate's degree. The Society of American Foresters recognizes forty-eight universities offering four-year degree programs and twenty-five colleges offering two-year associate's degrees. For a list of the forestry schools accredited by this organization, contact the Society of American Foresters (see Appendix A).

A bachelor's degree in range management or range science is the usual minimum educational requirement for range managers; graduate degrees are required for teaching and research positions.

Very few colleges offer degrees in soil conservation. Most soil conservationists hold degrees in agronomy, general agriculture, or crop or soil science.

## Finding That Job

Since most jobs in forestry and conservation are fairly specialized positions, they are often not advertised in your average Sunday classified ads. The Society of American Foresters maintains a list of resources to check for those seeking employment in these areas.

## Park Rangers

The National Park Service, a bureau under the U.S. Department of the Interior, administers more than 350 sites. These encompass natural and recreational areas across the country, including the Grand Canyon, Yellowstone National Park, and Lake Mead. Because most sites are not located near major cities, serious candidates must, for the most part, be prepared to relocate. Housing may or may not be provided, depending upon the site and the position.

The National Park Service hires three categories of park rangers at its sites, generally on a seasonal basis: enforcement, general, and interpretation. Most health nuts concerned with the environment apply for positions in the general category.

Duties vary greatly from position to position and site to site, but rangers in the general division are usually responsible for forestry or resource management; developing and presenting programs that explain a park's historic, cultural, or archeological features; campground maintenance; firefighting; lifeguarding; law enforcement; and search and rescue.

Rangers also sit at information desks, provide visitor services, or participate in conservation or restoration projects. Entry-level employees might also collect fees, provide first aid, and operate audiovisual equipment.

## Qualifications and Salaries

In determining a candidate's eligibility for employment, and at which salary level he or she would be placed, the National Park Service weighs several factors. Those with the least experience or education begin at the lowest federal government salary grade of GS-2 ($16,015). The requirements for that grade are only six months of experience in related work or a high school diploma or its equivalency.

The more related work experience or education, the higher the salary level. For example, GS-4 ($19,600 to $25,500) requires eighteen months of general experience in park operations or in related fields and six months of specialized experience; one ninety-day season as a seasonal park ranger is required at the GS-3 level ($17,474 to $22,712). Completion of two academic years of college may be substituted for experience if the course work covers related material.

Competition for jobs, especially at the most well-known sites, can be fierce, but the National Park Service employs a huge permanent staff, and this is supplemented tenfold by an essential seasonal workforce during peak visitation periods.

The best way for a newcomer to break in is to start with seasonal employment during school breaks. With a couple of summer seasons under your belt, the doors will open more easily for permanent employment. Because of Office of Personnel Management regulations, veterans of the U.S. Armed Forces have a definite advantage. Depending upon their experience, they may be given preference among applicants.

## How to Apply

Recruitment for summer employment begins September 1 with a January 15 deadline for applications. Some sites, such as Death Valley or Everglades National Park, also have a busy winter season. The winter recruitment period is June 1 through July 15. To apply for seasonal employment with the National Park Service, write to:

U.S. Department of the Interior
National Park Service Seasonal Employment Unit
P.O. Box 37127
Washington, DC 20013
www.nps.gov

You may also contact one of the ten regional offices of the National Park Service; the addresses are listed in Appendix A.

# Research and Education

Only through research and the passing on of accumulated knowledge can those concerned with the environment be effective in their jobs. Keeping the earth clean and healthy is a task that could never be accomplished without worldwide cooperation. The objectives seem unobtainable, the problems insurmountable—no one person or agency could do the work alone—but dedicated professionals find ways to contribute. Each project, each research station, each talk or presentation, each person educated makes an important contribution toward a healthy environment.

What follows are two examples of research and education centers dedicated to improving our environment.

## Lady Bird Johnson Wildflower Center

The Lady Bird Johnson Wildflower Center is the only national nonprofit research and educational organization committed to the preservation of native plants in planned landscapes. Founded in 1982 by Lady Bird Johnson, the Wildflower Center moved in 1995 from its location in a former hayfield east of Austin, Texas, to a new facility with thirty-four thousand square feet of buildings and seventy-two thousand square feet of display gardens and educational demonstration areas. It now covers forty-two acres of Texas hill country southwest of Austin where specialists conduct educational programs and research.

The Wildflower Center is dedicated exclusively to the study, preservation, and reestablishment of native plants in public and private landscapes. It strives to restore damaged habitats by sharing its knowledge and encouraging state highway departments, landscape architects and designers, developers, teachers, and backyard gardeners to use native plants.

These are some of the center's special facilities:

- Children's garden
- Meditation garden
- Observation tower
- Three greenhouses
- Theme gardens
- Research laboratory
- Three home-comparison gardens
- Volunteer workroom
- Rainwater collection and harvesting system
- Seed silo

The Wildflower Center generally employs professionals in the following positions:

- Executive director
- Editor
- Development director
- Education director
- Development associate
- Horticulturist
- Two or three support staff
- Two botanists
- Products manager
- Landscape manager
- Facility Sales manager
- Bookkeeper
- Public relations and marketing manager
- Records/membership manager

Because the Wildflower Center is nonprofit and funded privately, it relies heavily on the help of more than two hundred volunteers. Activities range from hosting fund-raisers to designing curricula for science teachers. Volunteering at this center and others like it is an excellent way for those concerned with the environment to acquire some practical hands-on training in a number of different disciplines. For more information contact:

Lady Bird Johnson Wildflower Center
4801 La Crosse Avenue
Austin, TX 78739
www.wildflower.org

## World Forestry Center

The World Forestry Center was originally built in 1905 as the Forestry Center for the Lewis and Clark Exposition held in Portland, Oregon. Its beautiful log cabin and all of its contents were destroyed by fire in 1964. The Western Forestry Center was reconstructed in 1971 and renamed the World Forestry Center in 1986.

The World Forestry Center is an educational organization aiming to increase understanding of the importance of well-managed forests and their related resources. Through its publications, educational programs, exhibits, and architecture, the center demonstrates the benefits of conserving the forest environment.

The World Forestry Center is also dedicated to the conservation of soil, trees, wildlife, water, and other natural resources. It accomplishes its mission through scientific research, demonstrations, and the distribution of forestry information. For more information about all the varied programs and volunteering opportunities, contact:

World Forestry Center
4033 Southwest Canyon Road
Portland, OR 97221
www.worldforestry.org

## Environmental Engineers

It's a dirty job, but someone has to do it. Cleaning up the environment, that is. Why not you? Health nuts concerned with environmental issues can enter careers in waste management and pollution control. And be well paid, too. There are a number of specialties in the field:

- **Air Quality Engineers.** Air quality engineers can have a variety of duties, but they are primarily problem solvers and researchers. They visit sites to investigate trouble areas, make improvement recommendations, and sometimes even enforce compliance. To reduce pollution, they can work as consultants on new construction projects or design new pollution-reducing devices or procedures.
- **Civil Engineers.** Civil engineering is the oldest branch of engineering. Civil engineers design and supervise the

construction of roads, airports, tunnels, bridges, buildings, and water supply and sewage systems. Specialties within civil engineering are water resource, environmental, construction, transportation, structural, and geotechnical engineering. Civil engineers usually work near major industrial and commercial centers, often at construction sites. Some projects are even located in remote areas or foreign countries.

- **Oil Pollution Control Engineers.** Wherever there is oil, there is the potential for an oil spill. Oil pollution control engineers try to prevent spills, but if the worst has already happened, they become involved with the cleanup process. Oil pollution control engineers generally work under emergency conditions. They have to make split-second decisions, taking into account wind direction, tides, or water currents. They also have to coordinate the efforts of a variety of involved agencies, such as wildlife protection organizations and local fire departments.

- **Sanitary Engineers.** Sanitary engineers work with water pollution control, water supply problems, and sewage disposal. Wherever there are problems, sanitary engineers investigate, taking and evaluating samples. Sanitary engineers also make recommendations about industrial concerns, sometimes designing waste treatment programs.

- **Waste Management Engineers.** While sanitary engineers deal with water and sewage problems, waste management engineers are concerned with solid waste management and cleanup of hazardous waste. They examine plans for disposal facilities, develop programs to make disposal more efficient, and conduct on-site inspections, often conferring with related health officials.

## Training

Engineers need to earn at least a bachelor's degree; many go on for a master's or even a doctorate. Bachelor's programs can take from four to five years to complete. Many of the specialties listed above require that the engineer be cross-trained. For example, an oil pollution control engineer would combine several disciplines, such as petroleum, chemical, and civil engineering. Sanitary engineers would earn a bachelor's in civil engineering, then specialize in sanitation at the master's level. The more areas you can specialize in within engineering, the more job situations are open to you.

## Salaries

Engineers enjoy the distinction of having the highest starting salaries of any bachelor's degree–level profession. Although salaries vary branch by branch, median annual earnings of environmental engineers in 2000 were $57,880. Civil engineers made a median $55,740. Starting salaries for new B.S. engineering graduates were slightly more than $51,000, a survey by the National Association of Colleges and Employers found in 2001. What you may expect to earn depends on the area of the country in which you live and whether you work in a government position or for private industry.

For further information on these engineering careers, as well as the technician and specialist jobs that support the profession, you can write to the professional associations listed in Appendix A or refer to the *Occupational Outlook Handbook,* listed in Appendix C.

......................................

# Environmentalists

In the field of environmentalism, there are a growing number of advocacy organizations that hire full-time staff. Many are based in Washington, D.C., where they keep an eye on the legislative process in Congress, work with government regulatory agencies, and meet with their constituencies. You have heard of many of these, such as the Sierra Club, National Wildlife Fund, and Nature Conservancy, among others. Some are politically moderate and focus on working through the system, while others pursue a more radical agenda for change. Greenpeace is probably the best-known example of a group that pursues its advocacy in the radical tradition, literally to the ends of the earth, in support of whales or to stop polluters. Organizing environmental advocacy programs requires administrators, lawyers, scientists, and others. It can and has formed the basis for entire careers. It's difficult to give an exact account of job options, educational requirements, and salaries in the field of environmentalism, which is not easily tracked by government statistics. You can research some of these organizations at websites such as www.eco.org or www.idealist.org, which provide lists of philanthropic organizations that include a number of environmental groups. The sites are organized with a useful search function. Find organizations that appeal to you and get an idea from their human resources staff what options may be open to someone with your talents.

Many universities are opening programs in environmental studies that promise to be good educational credentials for future environmental professionals. Your choice depends on your vision of the future. If it's cleaner oceans, you may head to Hawaii Pacific University for its environmental studies program in marine biology. If it's forests you're passionate about, you may be off to University of Oregon, which offers an undergraduate and graduate major in environmental studies with course work in global climate change and forest biology.

## Salaries and Outlook

You can often get a start as a volunteer, learning the ropes in an unpaid position. Salaries in paid positions range from $20,000 for clerical help to $40,000 or $50,000 for executive directors and environmental scientists and on up to six-figure salaries collected by the top executives of the leading environmental groups.

At the turn of the century the number of international nongovernmental organizations (NGOs) had grown to twenty-six thousand, according to a survey by the *Economist*, from six thousand a decade earlier. One of the biggest growth categories was environmental action and organizing. Clearly, it is a career universe open to talent.

# Professional Associations

For information about any of the careers highlighted throughout this book, and many others, write to the professional associations listed below. Most organizations offer prepared pamphlets and information packets, including up-to-date salary figures, education requirements, and job outlooks.

## Healers and Caregivers

American Academy of Nurse Practitioners
P.O. Box 12846
Austin, TX 78711
www.aanp.org

American College of Nurse-Midwives
818 Connecticut Avenue NW, Suite 900
Washington, DC 20006
www.midwife.org

American College of Sports Medicine (ACSM)
Member and Chapter Services Department
401 West Michigan Street
Indianapolis, IN 46202
www.acsm.org
   *ACSM Certification Resource Center for personal trainers and other sports medicine occupations can be found at www.lww.com/acsmcrc.*

American Nurses Association
600 Maryland Avenue SW, Suite 100 West
Washington, DC 20024
www.nursingworld.org

American Psychological Association
750 First Street NE
Washington, DC 20002
www.apa.org

Association of Child and Adolescent Psychiatric Nursing
1211 Locust Street
Philadelphia, PA 19107
www.ispn-psych.org

Association of Women's Health, Obstetric, and Neonatal Nurses
2000 L Street NW, Suite 740
Washington, DC 20036
www.awhonn.org

National Association of Orthopedic Nurses
Orthopedic Certification Board
401 North Michigan Avenue, Suite 2200
Chicago, IL 60611
www.orthonurse.org

Society of Education and Research in Psychiatric–Mental
    Health Nursing
1211 Locust Street
Philadelphia, PA 19107
www.ispn-psych.org

# Healing with Plants

American Herbalist Guild
1931 Gaddis Road
Canton, GA 30115
www.americanherbalistsguild.com
> *The American Herbalist Guild publishes a recommended reading list
> and a Web directory that lists a variety of training programs for
> herbalist careers.*

American Horticultural Therapy Association
909 York Street
Denver, CO 80206
www.ahta.org

Flower Essence Society
P.O. Box 459
Nevada City, CA 95959
www.flowersociety.org

Friends of Horticultural Therapy
909 York Street
Denver, CO 80206
www.ahta.org

Herb Research Foundation
4140 Fifteenth Street
Boulder, CO 80304
www.herbs.org

...............................

# Let's Get Physical

American Association for Leisure and Recreation (AALR)
1900 Association Drive
Reston, VA 22091
www.aahperd.org
> *The AALR publishes information sheets on twenty-five different careers in parks and recreation.*

American Camping Association
5000 State Road 67 North
Martinsville, IN 46151
www.acacamps.org
> *Contact the American Camping Association for information on careers in camping and summer counselor opportunities.*

American College of Sports Medicine (ACSM)
Member and Chapter Services Department
401 West Michigan Street
Indianapolis, IN 46202
www.acsm.org
> *ACSM provides certification for personal trainers.*

American Council on Exercise (ACE)
4851 Paramount Drive
San Diego, CA 92123
www.acefitness.org
> *ACE provides certification for personal trainers.*

American Occupational Therapy Association
4720 Montgomery Lane
P.O. Box 31220
Bethesda, MD 20824
www.aota.org

American Physical Therapy Association
1111 North Fairfax Street
Alexandria, VA 22314
www.apta.org

American Therapeutic Recreation Association
1414 Prince Street, Suite 204
Alexandria, VA 22314
www.atra-tr.org

Cruise Line International Association
500 Fifth Avenue, Suite 1407
New York, NY 10110
www.cruising.org

National Council for Therapeutic Recreation Certification
7 Elmwood Drive
New City, NY 10956
www.nctrc.org

National Recreation and Park Association
National Therapeutic Recreation Society
Division of Professional Services
22377 Belmont Ridge Road
Ashburn, VA 20148
www.nrpa.org

> *The National Recreation and Park Association provides information on career options and academic programs in the fields of recreation and recreational therapy.*

YMCA of the USA
101 North Wacker Drive
Chicago, IL 60606
www.ymca.net

# The World of Food

American Dietetic Association
120 South Riverside Plaza, Suite 2000
Chicago, IL 60606
www.eatright.org

American Farm Bureau Federation
225 Touhy Avenue
Park Ridge, IL 60068
www.fb.com

American Farmland Trust
1200 Eighteenth Street NW, Suite 800
Washington, DC 20036
www.farmland.org

American Society of Agronomy
677 South Segoe Road
Madison, WI 53711
www.agronomy.org

American Society of Farm Managers and Rural Appraisers
950 South Cherry Street, Suite 508
Denver, CO 80246
www.asfmra.org

Cooperative State Research, Education, and Extension Service
U.S. Department of Agriculture
1400 Independence Avenue SW
Washington, DC 20250
www.reeusda.gov
   *For an "ag careers" booklet, go to www.USDA.gov/da/employ/*
   *director.htm. For more on USDA careers, go to www.usajobs.gov.*

Crop Society of America
677 South Segoe Road
Madison, WI 53711
www.crops.org

Institute of Food Technologists
525 West Van Buren Street, Suite 1000
Chicago, IL 60607
www.ift.org

National Association of State Departments of Agriculture
1156 Fifteenth Street NW, Suite 1020
Washington, DC 20005
www.nasda-hq.org

National Farmers Union
11900 East Cornell Avenue
Aurora, CO 80014
www.nfu.org

National Future Farmers of America Organization
P.O. Box 68960
6060 FFA Drive
Indianapolis, IN 46268
www.ffa.org

North American Farm Alliance
P.O. Box 2502
Ames, IA 50010

Northeast Organic Farming Association
P.O. Box 697
Richmond, VT 05477
www.nofavt.org

...............................

# The Health Beat

American Booksellers Association
828 South Broadway
Tarrytown, NY 10591
www.bookweb.org

American Society of Journalists and Authors
1501 Broadway
New York, NY 10036
www.asja.org

American Society of Magazine Editors
919 Third Avenue, Twenty-Second Floor
New York, NY 10022
www.asme.magazine.org

American Society of Media Photographers
150 North Second Street
Philadelphia, PA 19106
www.asmp.org

Association of Authors' Representatives (AAR)
P.O. Box 237201
Ansonia Station
New York, NY 10003
www.aar-online.org

Author's Guild
31 East Twenty-Eighth Street, Tenth Floor
New York, NY 10016
www.authorsguild.org

The Dow Jones Newspaper Fund
P.O. Box 300
Princeton, NJ 08543
www.dowjones.com
*The Fund offers summer reporting and editing internships.*

National Newspaper Association
129 Neff Annex
University of Missouri—Columbia
Columbia, MO 65211
www.nna.org

National Press Photographers Association (NPPA)
3200 Croasdaile Drive, Suite 306
Durham, NC 27705
www.nppa.org
*The NPPA runs a job information bank and has regional and national divisions for professionals, students, and minorities.*

National Writers Union
113 University Plaza, Sixth Floor
New York, NY 10003
www.nwu.org

Newspaper Association of America
1921 Gallows Road, Suite 600
Vienna, VA 22182
www.naa.org

P.E.N. American Center
568 Broadway, Fourth Floor
New York, NY 10012
www.pen.org

# Healing the Environment

American Chemical Society
Education Division
1155 Sixteenth Street NW
Washington, DC 20036
www.chemistry.org

American Forests
P.O. Box 2000
Washington, DC 20013
www.americanforests.org

American Planning Association
122 South Michigan Avenue, Suite 1600
Chicago, IL 60603
www.planning.org

American Society of Civil Engineers
1801 Alexander Bell Drive
Reston, VA 20191
www.asce.org

American Society of Landscape Architects
636 Eye Street NW
Washington, DC 20001
www.asla.org

American Water Resources Association
4 West Federal Street
P.O. Box 1626
Middleburg, VA 20018
www.awra.org

Association of State and Interstate Water Pollution Control
Administration
750 First Street NE, Suite 1010
Washington, DC 20002
www.asiwpca.org

Bureau of Land Management
Office of Public Affairs
1849 C Street NW, Room 406-LS
Washington, DC 20240
www.blm.gov

Clean Water Action
4455 Connecticut Avenue NW, Suite A300
Washington, DC 20008
www.cleanwateraction.org

Colonial Williamsburg
Employment Office
P.O. Box 1776
Williamsburg, VA 23187
www.colonialwilliamsburg.org

Council of Landscape Architectural Registration Boards
144 Church Street NW, Suite 201
Vienna, VA 22180
www.clarb.org

JETS: The Junior Engineering Technical Society
1420 King Street, Suite 405
Alexandria, VA 22314
www.jets.org
   *JETS is a clearinghouse of information on engineering professions
   geared toward high school students.*

Lady Bird Johnson Wildflower Center
4801 Lacrosse Avenue
Austin, TX 78739
www.wildflower.org

National Park Service Headquarters
1849 C Street NW
Washington, DC 20240
www.nps.gov

National Park Service
Alaska Regional Office
2525 Gambell Street, Room 107
Anchorage, AK 99503

National Park Service
Pacific West Regional Office
One Jackson Center
1111 Jackson Street, Suite 700
Oakland, CA 94607

National Park Service
Intermountain Regional Office
12795 Alameda Parkway
Denver, CO 80225

National Park Service
Midwest Regional Office
1709 Jackson Street
Omaha, NE 68102

National Park Service
Southeast Regional Office
100 Alabama Street SW
1924 Building
Atlanta, GA 30303

National Park Service
Northeast Regional Office
U.S. Custom House
200 Chestnut Street, Fifth Floor
Philadelphia, PA 19106

National Park Service
National Capital Regional Office
1100 Ohio Drive SW
Washington, DC 20242

Natural Resources Conservation Service
Attn: Conservations Communications Staff
P.O. Box 2890
Washington, DC 20013
www.nrcs.usda.gov
> *This organization was formerly known as the Soil Conservation
> Service.*

National Wildlife Federation
11100 Wildlife Center Drive
Reston, VA 20190
www.nwf.org

Society of American Foresters
5400 Grosvenor Lane
Bethesda, MD 20814
www.safnet.org

Student Conservation Association (SCA)
689 River Road
Charlestown, NH 03603
www.thesca.org
> *SCA publishes an E-newsletter and offers information about
> conservation careers.*

U.S. Environmental Protection Agency
Ariel Rios Building
1200 Pennsylvania Avenue NW
Mail Code 3213A
Washington, DC 20460
www.epa.gov

U.S. Forest Service
P.O. Box 96090
Washington, DC 20090
www.fs.fed.us

Water Environment Federation
601 Wythe Street
Alexandria, VA 22314
www.wef.org

World Forestry Center
4033 Southwest Canyon Road
Portland, OR 97221
www.worldforestry.org

# Selected Training Programs

W rite to the following organizations for information about training programs in the many career areas discussed throughout the book. Many listed here are professional associations that offer specific information about educational programs recognized or recommended by the associations.

Society of American Foresters
5400 Grosvenor Lane
Bethesda, MD 20814
www.safnet.org
> *The Society of American Foresters recognizes forty-six universities offering four-year degree programs and twenty-one universities offering two-year associate's degrees.*

American Herbalist Guild
1931 Gaddis Road
Canton, GA 30115
www.americanherbalistsguild.com
> *The guild publishes a Web directory of training programs.*

American Horticultural Therapy Association (AHTA)
909 York Street
Denver, CO 80206
www.ahta.org
> *The website offers links to educational programs in horticultural therapy associated with AHTA and its certification program.*

Cleveland Botanical Garden
11030 East Boulevard
Cleveland, OH 44106
www.cbgarden.org
> *The Cleveland Botanical Garden offers a six-month internship program.*

Edmonds Community College
20000 Sixty-Eighth Avenue West
Lynnwood, WA 98036-5999
www.edcc.edu
> *Edmonds Community College offers a two-year program in horticultural therapy.*

Kansas State University
Department of Horticulture, Forestry, and Recreation Services
2021 Throckmorton Hall
Manhattan, KS 66506
www.ksu.edu
> *Kansas State University offers B.S. and M.S. programs in horticultural therapy.*

Rutgers University
Plant Science Department
Foran Hall, 59 Dudley Road
New Brunswick, NJ 08901
www.rutgers.edu
> *Rutgers offers a specialization in horticulture therapy.*

Temple University
Department of Landscape Architecture and Horticulture
Ambler, PA 19002
www.temple.edu/ambler/la-hort
> *Temple University offers upper-division courses in horticultural therapy and related therapy skills.*

Tennessee Technological University
School of Agriculture
Box 5034
Cookerville, TN 38505
www.tntech.edu
*The university offers horticultural therapy electives.*

University of Massachusetts
Department of Plant and Soil Sciences
Durfee Conservatory, French Hall
Amherst, MA 01002
www.umass.edu/plsoils

Virginia Polytechnic Institute and State University
  (Virginia Tech)
Department of Horticulture
401D Saunders Hall
Blacksburg, VA 24061
www.hort.vt.edu/undergraduate/undergraduate.htm
*Virginia Tech offers horticultural therapy B.S. and M.S. programs.*

Way to Grow, Inc.
164 Broad Street
Schuylerville, NY 12871
www.horticulturaltherapy.org
*This organization offers an internship program.*

# Further Reading

*Careers for Nature Lovers & Other Outdoor Types*, by Louise
  Miller, VGM Career Books, Chicago IL.
*Careers for Shutterbugs & Other Candid Types*, by Cheryl
  McLean, VGM Career Books, Chicago IL.
*Careers for Writers & Others Who Have a Way with Words*, by
  Robert W. Bly, VGM Career Books, Chicago, IL.
*Guide to Literary Agents* (annual), Writer's Digest Books,
  Cincinnati, OH.
*How to Get a Job with a Cruise Line*, by Mary Fallon Miller,
  Ticket to Adventure Publishing, St. Petersburg, FL.
*How to Write a Book Proposal*, by Michael Larsen, Writer's Digest
  Books, Cincinnati, OH.
*How to Write Irresistible Query Letters*, by Lisa Collier Cool,
  Writer's Digest Books, Cincinnati, OH.
*Occupational Outlook Handbook* (annual), Bureau of Labor
  Statistics, U.S. Department of Labor, Washington, DC.
*Opportunities in Forestry Careers*, by Christopher M. Wille, VGM
  Career Books, Chicago, IL.
*Opportunities in Occupational Therapy Careers*, by Marguerite
  Abbott, Marie-Louise Franciscus, and Zona R. Weeks, VGM
  Career Books, Chicago IL.
*Opportunities in Physical Therapy Careers*, by Bernice
  Krumhansl, VGM Career Books, Chicago, IL.
*Opportunities in Sports and Fitness Careers*, by Wm. Ray
  Heitzmann, VGM Career Books, Chicago, IL.

*Photographer's Market* (annual), Writer's Digest Books, Cincinnati, OH.

*Writer's Market* (annual), Writer's Digest Books, Cincinnati, OH.

*Your Personal Trainer*, by Douglas Brooks, Human Kinetics, Champaign, IL.

# About the Author

A s a full-time writer of career books, Blythe Camenson is primarily concerned with helping job seekers make educated choices. She firmly believes that with enough information, readers can find long-term, satisfying careers. To that end, she researches traditional as well as unusual occupations, talking to a variety of professionals about what their jobs are really like. In all of her books she includes firsthand accounts from people who can reveal what to expect in each occupation, the upsides as well as the down.

Camenson's interests range from history and photography to writing novels. She is also director of Fiction Writer's Connection, a membership organization providing support to new and published writers.

Camenson was educated in Boston, earning her bachelor of arts degree in English and psychology from the University of Massachusetts and her master's degree in counseling and education from Northeastern University. She has had several careers herself, including career and educational counselor, psychotherapist, and English as a foreign language teacher.

Blythe Camenson is also the author of *How to Sell, Then Write Your Nonfiction Book* (Contemporary Books).